ARRIVAL PRESS

KITCHEN KAPERS

Edited

By

TIM SHARP

First published in Great Britain in 1996 by
ARRIVAL PRESS
1 - 2 Wainman Road, Woodston,
Peterborough, PE2 7BU

HB ISBN 1 85786 442 5
SB ISBN 1 85786 437 9

Foreword

Think of the time you had a culinary disaster and how you dealt with it.

Well that's what this anthology is all about; the day the lid fell of the salt pot, the saucepan boiled dry, the soufflé that didn't rise.

Whilst editing this book I realised that I'm not the only one who has the odd cooking calamity.

Kitchen Kapers brings together all of these disasters in poetic form to give you a very entertaining and amusing read.

Tim Sharp
Editor

CONTENTS

DEVOTED TO THE FRYER

We have a lovely big kitchen and all the mod cons,
but out of all the many dishes we eat sausages by the ton.
They say junk food is bad,
but it's all we've ever had.
Time after time out comes the fryer
and in go the chips as the heat gets higher.
Six plates are spread,
along with lashings of bread.
Steep with low fat butter
most folk would chuck in the gutter.
But a meal is a meal, I know it makes us fat
so out comes the fryer for us and Aunty Pat.
But our huge mod cons kitchen would not be complete,
if it wasn't for the fryer, we'd fall down on our feet.

Trevor Barnes

PUDDING DISASTER

Have you ever made a pudding
that seemed to go all wrong
when family turn around and say
'Oh what's that awful pong?'
You serve it up so lovingly
but all they do is frown
you forgot to put the sugar in
and the topping's black not brown.
You've washed the bowl
you've soaked and scrubbed
but it just won't come out clean
it couldn't have been greased first
all you want to do is scream.
Next time you want a pudding
and your heart is filled with dread
don't get out the pudding bowl
pop out and buy one instead.

Dorothy Johnstone

THE FOOD FIGHT

Marmite, Marmite everywhere,
On her blouse and in her hair,
But Alison is so well liked
Mark had better run for his life.

Some curry flew into Mark's face,
Leo said it was a disgrace,
He cooked the curry for an hour
Trying hard not to make it sour.

A funny thing to try to do,
To put yoghurt into Mark's shoe.
And while he was dealing with that
A raw egg on his head went splat.

The sign that says, 'No food fights'
Is covered now in egg and rice.
This is Mark's very worst bad dream,
Someone's got a tub of ice cream.

Malcolm Lisle

A USELESS COOK

Cooking in the kitchen, for me,
Is like falling out of a tree,
All that I make gets burnt,
And I still haven't learnt
Why they call it dinner, supper and tea.

I need someone who'll supervise,
Someone who's alert and'll keep open their eyes,
'Cause if something starts smoking,
We'll all end up choking,
And be left with cremated dried pies.

Even my daughter supervised me one day,
Hoping I wouldn't go too far astray,
I forgot to pierce the spuds,
All I heard was a thud,
I cleaned the oven for the rest of the day.

It was a Saturday I decided to bake
A wonderfully spongy sponge cake,
I went and used plain,
Thought self-raising was the same,
Now that was my flat mistake.

I've decided the kitchen's not for me,
I'm going to leaving cooking be,
I've hung my apron up,
Poured coffee in my cup,
Arghh! Now I've spilt that over me.

Richard Bright

CULINARY CATASTROPHES

Tonight I must make a special meal
My in-laws are coming to dine.
I search the supermarket shelves
For all the ingredients and wine.

I have seen all the chefs on the tele,
From them I have gleaned a few tips.
I take out the pans and utensils,
From a wine glass I take a few sips.

Now to bone and skin chicken portions,
Chop the garlic, peppers and chives.
The spuds and veg I start to prepare
Dash! My finger I've cut with the knife.

I cover my cut with a plaster,
Take a few more sips of wine.
The casserole goes in the oven
It should be ready in time.

As I begin to make a sweet sauce
To cover the fresh fruit flan
I answer the phone and start chatting,
Forget the sauce, it's now stuck to the pan!

My best crockery lays on the table
Though two plates I chipped, almost broke.
My pan with the sauce burnt and sticky
Lies in hot soapy water to soak.

The in-laws are ringing the doorbell,
At least the casserole seems to be fine.
With luck they won't notice the two cracked plates,
Burnt pan, and half empty bottle of wine!

Barbara Sowden

BROWN BLOBS

From off the shelf
I took this mix,
Not just for two
But enough for six.

Into a basin I
Tossed the lot.
Just add an egg
And one for the pot!

Heat up the oven,
When that is done
Grease two tins
Pour in the gunge.

Nearly time to
Look and test,
Before I serve
Same to my guests.

I open up but
To my horror,
Big brown blobs
Heave up and over.

Forming shapes of
Brown it made,
As over the shelves
It did cascade.

What have I done
For my cake to lunge?
This is supposed to be
A chocolate sponge.

Beryl Smyter

KITCHEN CAPERS

My kitchen is a place of fun
Especially when my grandchildren come
To pass time on a rainy day
To my kitchen they go to bake

Drew his sponge cakes happily bakes
Eats more mix than goes into his cakes
Into the cake cups full to the top
Into my oven heavily dropped

Out in ten minutes lovely and brown
Put on a plate to let them cool down
Covered in icing cherry on top
Into his mouth they soon will all pop

Erin is four ever so proud
Will help in my kitchen happy for hours
Crispies she bakes full of chocolate and butter
Into little cases they gone one another
Into the fridge to take them out
They taste lovely but left lying about

Ross who is three makes rabbits for you and me
Into the shapes chocolate he pours
More on his face hands and floor
Licks the spoon scrapes the bowl
Into the freezer to make them cold
After a while out they come shares them out with everyone

Sponge cakes mix crispies on the floor
Chocolate mix mess galore
Not like my kitchen any more
Tidy up put things away use again another day
To my kitchen I say this prayer
Thanks dear kitchen for being there.

Maureen E Smith

CHOCOLATE SURPRISE

My little grandson came to stay
He loves to help me so
Loves it in the kitchen
Just can never tell him no

He wanted us to make a cake
Thought chocolate was the best
Suddenly the phone rang
Grant thought he would mix the rest

Dear little soul had chocolate mouth
And chocolate ears and nose
In fact was really plastered
From hair to tiny toes

He thought the dog looked hungry
Said it could have a lick
But gave it just a bit too much
And made the poor dog sick

Little chocolate hand prints
On every kitchen door
Contented chocolate covered dog
Sleeping on the floor

The chocolate mix looks much too dark
I will fix it Nan, for you
So quickly found the jug of cream
And poured that all in too

Now let this be a lesson
When you are talking on the phone
Never leave your grandson
Making chocolate cake alone

Angela Pearson

ONIONS TO YOU

Ho no!
Not again,
Dad, your Sunday lunch
Is always the same.

Ho no!
Your Yorkshire pud
Just won't rise.
Look! It just rolled
Over and died.

Ho no!
Your roast beef
Just fell off the bone.

Ho no!
Your toad retreated
And ran back down the hole.

Ho no!
Jam roly-poly,
Look! Girls, it's complete,
Ho dear! It's welded itself to your teeth.

Ho no!
Sorry girls, it's bangers with mash.
Dad! It's always the same.

Ho no!
Why does my wife work every weekend?
Because
Claire and Marie
Always complain.

James Stewart

MY KIND OF CAPER

In my kitchen you will find
Capers of a different kind.

Crushed with brains they used to be
But that has gone with BSE.

Pork with capers, roast not stew,
(Never serve it to a Jew).

Pickled eggs to start the day
With capers, spice and leaf of bay.

Just in case you do not know
On a bush these capers grow.

In my kitchen you'll not find
Capers of that other kind.

B C Watts

IN A JAM

Home-made jam - a special treat
Blackcurrants galore growing at my feet
Now's the time to test my skill
And collect the jars, to the brim I'll fill.

With so much fruit the family deserve
To taste my special home preserve
I reach to the shelf for a cookery book
Then I take a long, long look.

It's a lot of fuss, but it'll be no crime
If I use the steamer to half the time
I fill the pan to a good, good measure
The next thing I know, it's under pressure.

My first attempt, I start to dream
When suddenly the kitchen's full of steam
I switch off the gas, take off the weight
Red steam escapes - it's much too late.

The ceiling turns pink, the walls to red
Hubby's due home, something I dread
We'll need fresh paint - curtains too
The cooker's burnt black - will a chisel do?

Maureen Pearce-Webb

THE FIRST ATTEMPT

'Wash up,' they said,
'you are big enough now,'
'I can't,' I cried, 'I don't know how'
I prodded the suds.
What do I do?
I emptied the bottle, the water turned blue.
I threw in some plates,
at least three or four,
I threw in a fifth
but it fell to the floor.
I looked down in shame,
it was mother's best set,
her face was a sight that
I will never forget.
'Leave it now, we will
do it ourselves, you're
not big enough yet,
but we'd like your help.'

Wayne Ford

WASHING UP

Suds in the sink, saucers and spoons
Knives, forks and delicate cup,
Plates, pudding basins and bowls,
Why is there so much washing up?
How many hours do I stand at the sink
Splashing the water so gaily?
But it gives me a chance to ponder and think
With so much washing up needed daily.

While I do the dishes my mind is elsewhere
Away on a far distant shore
Where they picnic on sands warm and soft
With no things to wash up anymore.

For they dine upon fruit, and fish from the sea
Cooked over sticks on fire bright,
There shells are pans with plates made from leaves
They just throw them away every night!

Now it's soak every saucepan, scrub every tin
Rinse the milk bottles, empty the bin,
Clean all the cutlery, polish the glasses,
Whilst washing up and daydreaming
How quickly the morning passes.

So I stand at the sink with rubber gloves on
With dish cloth, scouring pad and the Squeezy,
With so much to do I pretend it's a game,
When it's done, I'm the winner, that's easy.
Now the washing up's finished and all put away
The kitchen looks tidy and neat
Everything's ready again for next day
What a pity that folk need to eat!

Joan Heybourn

MY KITCHEN

Kettle always ready
to make a pot of tea,
cakes on the table
for friends who visit me,

a cake baking slowly
just about to rise,
dinner almost served
a sight for sore eyes.

Coffee or tea
perhaps some buttered toast?
A place to relax
and eat a Sunday roast,

peace and calm
a lovely place to be
biscuits and gossip
and a warm cup of tea.

Andrea Hazeldine

HOME COOKING

I find much joy cooking in my kitchen,
Forgetting all my troubles as I pitch in.
All the good cooks in their books alongside
Ready, willing and able to help, to guide.

I may try a stew, but first I kick out the cat,
Not much use as an ingredient that.
Now scrub the kitchen table, secure all doors.
No-one must disturb me - no-one at all.

Then I take up the meat, mince it so small,
It may well take me an hour to find it once more.
Take a nice large saucepan - this one will do.
It must, face it, I don't own two.

I start to weep. Oh what can the matter be?
Peeling onions always has that effect on me.
Now, what next to peel, dice or quarter.
Sounds so cruel - maybe I hadn't ought to.

Garrotte the carrots, split the peas. Give no quarter
Peel, chop and swiftly drown them in water.
I look for potatoes. Yes, I have a pound or two.
Decisions, decisions, how many to do?

Salt, pepper, herbs, spices, how my hands fly.
Parsnip, turnip, cabbage, never ask why.
Tomato, celery, anything I can see,
All into the pan to be stewed for me.

Press on, plenty more work to be done.
I could add dumplings, though soon I will be one.
I've just had a brainwave. I do have a few.
Two days it can last me my delicious stew.

Maureen Connelly

UNTITLED

A family meal was what was planned,
But everything went mad,
Spaghetti Bolognese was what we had,
Me, Sam, Mum and Dad.
Dad didn't like it,
Mum was not glad,
She threw her plate through the air,
And spaghetti landed on Dad's hair.
Dad didn't like it, he disagreed,
But then he threw food at me,
We were all at it, throwing food in the air,
Sam hid under a chair,
No one could get him there.
You should have seen it,
When we were done,
We left all the mess to Mum.

Amanda Jervis

KITCHEN CAPERS

My kitchen is my favourite room
I make a mess, then just sweep up with a broom
Now I class myself a fairly good cook
But now and then, out comes my recipe book

But today's cooking uses more herbs and spice
Which I like to try, and find quite nice
So I ventured out, to do my first curry
But alas, I think I was too much in a hurry

Too much garlic, not enough herbs
Lacking in spices, otherwise - superb?
I thought don't give in, try another day
Then chuck everything in, come what may

It turned out quite good, just the right taste
So none of it went in the dustbin as waste
So back in my kitchen once more cooking
Mess on the floor, but who's looking

This time it's a cake I hope won't flop
If it does, into dustbin, out come mop
Well it came good
I guess I knew it would

Well this is my domain, I stir, mix, grill and roast
This is my kitchen, where I play host
For my family and friends. I do a meal
This makes me feel good, that's how I feel

Jean Linney

KITCHENITIS

We've all got *kitchenitis*
A complaint so very severe,
Our minds are really quite scrambled,
And we'll never recover I fear.

All our friends and relations are worried,
'Come to see us, they say. 'Have some fun.'
But we shake our heads and say once again,
'We will when the kitchen is done.'

We've been saying this now for more than six weeks,
Our conversation will bore you to tears,
'Just the tiles to finish and the floor to be done,
And we've wood shavings right up to our ears!'

The children are thirsty and grubby,
We've turned the water off at the main,
'Cause the sink and taps have got to be moved,
Will we ever be normal again?

I'm sure that we're turning neurotic.
'Mind the paint, watch the wood,' we both howl,
There's nowhere to prepare any dinner,
And *Polyurethene-Matt* smells quite foul.

But when the kitchen is finally finished,
it will be our salvation, our cure,
-But the bedrooms are all looking shabby,
We'll have *bedroomitis* next month, that's for sure!

Susan Wooden

MAKING A CAKE

To produce a perfect cake,
One has to follow the set instruction
To the letter, taking great care
With every step one takes.

Making a cake is not easy,
Nothing can be rushed,
Towards getting the best results
For your perfect cake.

When each detail
Has been followed,
Nothing more to add,
Everything now waits
For the final outcome.

Yet it's all left to chance
We all have to take,
Having a bit of luck helps,
With all the aspect involved.

Lady luck is not always with us,
Win or fail,
Luck has a lot to play.
That is why we never make
The perfect cake every time.

Diane Godbold

TOO MANY COOKS

Too many cooks in our house
Or it often seems that way,
Whenever something's on the stove
They all must have their say.

That could do with just a pinch of salt
This curry needs more spice,
Those Yorkshire puds will turn out flat
A touch bicarb will make them nice.

Shall I stir your oriental fry
I'll just have a little taste,
Will you leave that Sunday roast alone
It's already had a baste.

Then what's left is dirty pots and pans
But will anyone wash or dry,
The mere mention of these menial tasks
Well, they do say pigs can fly.

Too many cook I do believe
Invariably spoil the broth,
And when it comes to washing up
Those cooks won't lift a cloth.

James C Watt

DISHWASHER

Said my daughter to hubby,
'The dishes are grubby
And they're all piled high in the sink.
Don't just sit there all bloated,
Because we've now voted
It's your turn to get your hands pink.'

'Just wait a minute,' he sighed,
'And I'll do them with pride.
But just now I need a short nap!.
You'll have met the kind before,
They hate washing up chore,
When asked they turn all *Andy Capp*!

Almost half an hour passes,
Time for demi-tasses,
And hubby's still snoring away.
'Will you get off your rear end,
To the kitchen your way wend,
For sleeping just call it a day!'

Son-in-law appeals mildly,
(Needs an ally wildly),
'I'm sure with Jim you'd no trouble?'
'No! I never did,' I said,
'Not all the time we were wed,
But son - you're sure not his double!'

I didn't have to prompt him,
Nor say 'Come on' to Jim,
In fact nothing too dramatic.
After we'd eaten dinner
He was a sure winner . . .
A dish washer automatic!

E Balmain

A KITCHEN PRAYER

Take two cups of happiness
A cup of laughter do,
Season well with love and hope
A pinch of goodness too.
Add a cup of faithfulness
Then mix with patience long
Sprinkle now with joy and peace
A ray of sunshine strong.
Share this food with warmth and grace
In kind and gentle ways.
Tenderness and hands that care
Such blessings all our days.

Margaret Jackson

FRANTIC COOK

It is half past three in the afternoon,
the cook gets ready, bowl, scales and wooden spoon.
Deciding on, what to bake,
how about a vegan cake.

'I need a baking bowl,' the cook shouts out,
the tidy kitchen is just about
to become a mess, left in her hands,
like the bombed areas of now destitute lands.

Mixer switched on, such a noise,
but this is one of the cook's handy toys.
Buzzing sounds echo in the room
and all needed is a bang, bang, boom.

Talking to herself, brain now in control,
singing out of key, an unmelodic bellow,
too much noise, now a sudden hush
the cook takes it easy, no need to rush.

Rinse the raisins, drop them into the bowl,
mixture now ready, time to roll.
Flour the board, some on the floor.
'Where has the flour gone? Need some more.'

A distant bark, a trumpet sound,
game of cards, the cook looks round,
door closes, cooks moves to oven,
light's gone out, 'Ready in ten.'

Whilst waiting for mixture to bake,
cook rattles up another cake.
You see once she gets started
there is no turning back,
baking, more baking in heaps and stacks.

Adele E McCafferty

MY FRIEND IN THE KITCHEN

It was in the kitchen I first saw,
Through babies' eyes so many things to explore,

All of which were bigger than me it seemed
And where every utensil smiled a garnished gleam!

The warmest friend I found in the kitchen stood big and bold,
White in colour and its presence far from cold,

It was to me the finest of them all yes, so hot,
The magical way it could produce things from any old pot.

I watched with scrambled thoughts as it again went to bake,
And this time it made the world's most delicious cake!

Debra Neale

PANCAKES

Have you ever tried
To toss a pancake,
Take the plunge
And launch it in the air?

It looks so easy done by experts
Who toss without a care,
Manipulate the frying pan
Catching in mid air.

We had a go and
Laughed until we cried,
Our pancake failed to make it
Didn't reach inside.

Seizing on this piece of luck
A furry frame appeared
And scooped our pancake off the floor
Then vanished through the kitchen door.

No need to ask if he enjoyed it,
His wagging tail told all,
We'll have another go at tossing
And trust it doesn't hit the wall.

Jean Humphris

MARIGOLDS FOR SALE

The Free Ads advert reads 'Dishwasher for sale, slight attention it needs.'
Will it be money going down the drain? Or the answer to a chore that's
become a pain.
My problems could be solved, I'll rethink again.
The day will come when I'll have time to spare,
whether welcome or not I'll not know until I am there.
To do yourself out of thinking time,
when scraping the plates to get rid of the grime.
I think of us all and where our lives will lead,
of a trip to the supermarket and us four to feed.
Food to be bought, emptied out and cooked,
and a list of the items I've overlooked!
So once again, I'll let my mind wander
back to the Free Ads and again I ponder.
The question once more springs to mind.
Is dishwashing my time to sort out mankind?
Great thinkers of the world should unite,
wage war on those dishes and fight the good fight!
There's only one solution to the question I think.
Let's go back and revisit my overfilled sink.
Watching the water go down the drain,
I turn on the taps to start once again.
It makes things seem so simple somehow,
doing the dishes with the right know-how.
Look out! Natasha's back one more,
trying her luck, but the answer is still 'No.'
I think of the day when my experience and knowledge will be put into doubt,
of the inevitable words '*What do you know!*' she'll shout.
There is no point in dwelling, I try not to think
of a life with a dishwasher, and a redundant sink!

Karren Dawn Kinsey

RICE KRISPIES

Rice Krispies on a spoon is a bit of a bore,
So why not try to suck them through a straw,
If you give it a go, I wish you good luck,
And I hope halfway up they don't get stuck!

But if they do, all they need is a hard blow,
And when they unstick, you'll definitely know,
As in the milk there will be bubbles of air,
But don't laugh so much you fall off your chair!

Then if you want to be as silly as me,
And put the same straw back in your tea,
The Rice Krispies will float to the top,
And will no longer go snap, crackle or pop!

Helen Tilbury

ANIMATED GOODIES

I have moved quite recently
My kitchen is so small
I sometimes wonder ruefully
If I'm meant to cook at all.
But it isn't just the cooking
As I said the kitchen's small
And you can't have many cupboards
If you haven't got much wall.
So the cupboards tend to be quite full
And the contents come to life
A pack of muesli leapt from shelf
And struck me in the eye.
To retaliate I jammed it back
It nudged the Ovaltine,
This hit a jar of Marmite,
What a mess there could have been
If I hadn't caught it neatly,
Thus banging head on door.
Let's call a truce - if things stay put
I promise I will swear no more.

Kathleen Jarrold

KITCHEN SINK OPERA

Another dawn; another day;
Another round of tasks;
Another set of problems
Unsolvable, alas.

Another sink that's full of pots
All waiting to be washed;
Another shout of squabbling kids;
All hopes of quiet dashed.

Another day devoted to
Umpiring youthful folly;
Another bout of pushing round
A supermarket trolley.

And while I'm cleaning up one mess
They're building up another;
Won't pick a thing up off the floor
And who would be a mother?

Another trail of footprints on
A floor that I just washed;
And into next door's garden,
Another ball's been tossed.

There's kids and dogs and husband
All waiting to be fed;
To think of it makes me feel weak;
I think I'll stay in bed.

Sybil Sibthorpe

COOKING THE BOOKS

I was using it - me posh new pan - and I'd turned the ring up high.
It was a pan quite indispensable, and I knew the reason why.
It steamed , it fried, it kept things hot, how had I lived without it?
A meal for four? No problem! how could anybody doubt it?

Sniff, sniff - that's odd, a burning smell, horrid and quite strong.
Lift it off for a moment - surely there's something wrong.
No, all seems OK. Turn on again - there's nothing *to* go wrong.
It's funny though, that the burning smell is getting quite so strong.

Hey! A waft of smoke is pluming above the treasured pan.
Do something, somebody! Stop it if you can.
This time the pan is lifted off and taken well apart.
There in the hidden base we find what's burning from the start.

There, all charred and blackened, still burning a little flame,
Is the vital 'book of instructions' with which the pan first came.
Hurriedly they're snatched away and damped beneath the tap.
Thank goodness it happened in England - it's the *French* pages where
there's a gap!

Beryl Jones

KITCHEN CAPERS

At four thirty in the afternoon food flies everywhere,
Spaghetti smears the kitchen and banana on the chair.
And sitting at the table without a single care in the world,
Smothered in dinner are my three little girls.

Kellie demonstrates the use of milk rubbed in her face,
Whilst Louise smears spaghetti up the walls and all over the place.
Teri Anne wipes her dinner all over my newly cleaned walls
But when it comes to feeding time there's definitely no rules.

Then comes six and it's time to make their tea
As I look round my kitchen all clean and sparkly.
Making up their drinks of milk and spreading jam upon their bread
My daughters try my patience by pouring milk over their heads.

Oh, these kitchen capers bring to me some stress,
My once cleaned fitted kitchen now smothered in this mess.
Sticky little finger marks and rolls of kitchen paper,
No-one's safe at feeding time during Kitchen Capers.

Deborah Suzanne Child

IMPRESS

Neatly trimmed sandwiches of cucumber and cress
Fancy folded napkins with rings, we tried to impress

A china tea set was used, it was one of our best
The cutlery was neatly placed, for each and every guest

Silver stands adorned with cakes of every kind
Trying to impress, we chose the best we could find

Table cloths were imported, if asked that's what I would say
We bought them abroad, last year when we were away

Creamed scones and fruit jam placed in separate dishes
A kind of tea that's not for me and food that's against my wishes

When it was over, we stood looking, both at a loss
All this to please, trying to impress the boss

Sausage and mash, now that's my kind of fare
Feet up in front of the telly, relaxed in a chair

Roy Hunter

A SUNDAY DISASTER

As I read my book, it fell to the floor
I noticed a smell drifting through the door
Once again I'd burned the roast
I'm not a good cook, I don't like to boast

I'd burnt Sunday dinner, what should I do
Sardines on toast especially for two
Unfortunately, I couldn't open the tin
So the sardines went straight into the bin

No sardines, so then what could we eat
Toasted cheese, what a wonderful treat
Sadly there was absolutely no cheese
Why is this happening, please, help me, please

A culinary disaster, I have no bread
What, tell me, what can we have instead?
In my cupboard I have some jam
But no bread, keep calm, please keep calm

I'll send out for chips, or Chinese curry
But really there is no need to hurry
Time to read just a little bit more
Oh my God, my head is so sore

Time is really running out fast
My husband is home, blast, oh blast
But, what's that in his arms, what can I see
An Indian curry for him and for me

Oh why did I worry, ow why so much pain?
My husband can definitely do this again
You see in my haste I completely forgot
Today is my birthday, what a silly, silly clot

Ann Harrison

KITCHEN CAPERS

We've all read the scenario,
New kitchen, clean and posh,
A place for this, a place for that,
A place to cook the nosh.
The cooker's mighty different, though,
Electric now, not gas,
How *do* you read the numbered dial,
For chicken, beef or bass?
The ceiling spots are shining down,
On pans, and cups and wok,
All that we have to do now is
Uncork the fine, chilled Hock.
You celebrate the first *real* meal
Since alterations finished,
So let's have the menu one last time,
Optimism undiminished.
The sauce is done, (oh! No, it's not,
You've turned it down too low),
The soufflé's risen far too much,
(You should have cooked that slow!)
The carrots, still, are far too tough,
The roast potatoes charred,
The spinach, now, has turned to mush,
(This Cordon Bleu's too hard!)
Hold on a mo, think hard, think quick,
A number springs to mind,
That Take-Away, just down the road,
Should not be hard to find.
Turn everything off, give up for the present,
Order two meals (they just might do a pheasant!)

Terence Pemberton

THE TROUBLE WITH FOOD . . .

Is everything just looks so deliciously good,
When I look at the pictures in my recipe book,
There's Italian, Spanish, Chinese and Mexican,
The instructions look easy. Cook? Of course I can.

Now let me see what, from my book, can I make,
The decision is hard but I suppose I could even bake,
A picture caught my eye of a tempting chicken dish,
With vegetables and fries, and a creamy wine relish.

I quickly scan the instructions, perhaps I'm being brave,
Tsp(!) What's that? Gently brown(!) Fold in an egg(!)
On reflection of my cooking skills, I shouldn't really boast,
I hope no-one was starving, uhmm, anyone for toast?

Tracey Thomson

CULINARY SKILLS

It's cold outside, rain pouring down.
It's the kitchen for me, bake a cake for tea,
Warm and cosy, radio on, ingredients assembled,
What can go wrong?
The first egg I broke dropped on the floor,
It wasn't just that, it splashed up the door.

Now everything safely stirred up in the bowl,
Tin all greased, sides and all,
I put in the cake mixture and smoothed the top,
Into the oven, but not too hot.

I went to look after an hour or two,
It had risen nicely, now what to do?
Is it done? I'm not quite sure,
I had better hurry and shut the door.
When next I looked my cake had sunk,
Was it a reflection on the weather - who knows.
It was pouring with rain, it could know I suppose.

I must not despair, I'll try to repair
The disaster my cake had befallen,
So I cut out the middle and filled it with fruit,
Made some hot custard, oh what a hoot.
Now outside the sun it is shining.

Margaret Kinshott

KITCHEN DIY

We bought a new kitchen
I installed it myself
I'll give you this warning
It can damage your health

The cupboards were broken
My sink top was cracked
I tried levelling shelves up
Then damaged my back

I started to hammer
Then missed it my thumb
Sat down for a moment
'Ouch' a tack in my bum

The kitchen was white
With touches of red
From the blood that had spilled
Out of the gash in my head

There's no DIY from now on
I do promise because
This flippin' job
Nearly cost me my marriage

When it was finished
It looked pretty good
From the fridge in the corner
To the new hob and hood

So now take warning
And listen to me
Stick to the gardening
Or making the tea

Kenneth Mayoh

CHEDDAR TEARS

I'm having a mid-morning crisis,
the cooker has gone on the blink.
I was hoping to make rarebit slices,
but I'm blubbering into the sink!

The seconds on't clock begin racing,
leaving me far behind at the post.
The vicar and wife, how disgracing,
to offer them cheese but no toast!

Wait a mo' I think that I've cracked it,
as I recall that unwanted gift.
I climb down mucked up from the attic,
but my spirit is starting to lift!

It's one of those toast sandwich makers,
to cook them you don't need a stove!
They're ready in minutes for all takers,
'For small mercies I thank him above!'

The door bell commands that I answer,
and all is under control,
background music is in its first stanza
as I hang up their coats in the hall.

'Did I mention,' (sniffs vicar's wife sweetly)
'that the vicar and I never eat
cheese of any description . . . '
I felt the pain as my jaw hit my feet!

Dawn Hall

KITCHEN CHAOS

No-one wipes the worktops in the kitchen anymore
And if you look closely you'll see crumbs upon the floor!
The cooker top defies inspection . . . the oven's not worth a mention,
Drawers and cupboards on the walls are screaming for attention!

Gone are the days of morning rituals . . .
Wipe this . . . wash that . . . each blob of fat and last night's supper victuals
Are too mundane . . . but there again I'll have to do it later,
Preparing food is such a chore . . . a bore . . .a chaos creator!

There are tea stains rife inside the sink . . .
Doesn't anybody ever think
To rinse with water the morning's brew . . .
No, leave it to Mom, she's not got much to do!

But Mom's a poet . . . and would rather write
Than battle with the pots and pans . . . till night
When brood come home, all tired and weary,
She'll welcome them with greetings cheery!

Tasty smells all emanating . . . is it pizza or is it stew?
Is it sweet 'n' sour chicken or rough robust ragout?
No . . . it's Mom's concoction, just like her poems
That come spontaneously in appetising tones!

But always there's a glass of wine . . .
Dad's own vintage . . . but it's fine;
He says it's not had full ferment
But in making it he's a happy gent!

So overall I can't complain, it's happiness that counts,
When I look round my kitchen small I forget the dos and don'ts;
There's no vanity . . . it is sanitary . . . and keeping my sanity is best . . .
I'm not competing for a culinary prize, I'll leave that to the rest!

Jean Makin

KITCHEN CAPERS

Returning from my honeymoon, first time to make the dinner,
A cooked pie full of vegetables, it seemed to me a winner,
From the book I learned the recipe, repeating stage by stage,
Then I closed it and forgot it, and couldn't find the page,
I guessed the oven setting and then grated all the cheese,
And slipped upon some cooking fat, to bring me to my knees.

An egg rolled off the table, and ran swift across the floor,
I moved my foot to trap it, to crush it flatly by the door,
With four big sprigs of parsley, and a massive runner bean,
A leek and button mushrooms, the contents looked too green,
My clock then stopped its ticking, I was lost in space in time,
With the onion, cheese and egg yolk, the colour turned to lime.

The pastry fits the pie dish, with rolled flour, eggs and fat,
But like the egg it tumbled, and frightened off the cat.
The onions made my eyes red, my fingers clogged with flour,
The beaten egg and carrots somehow made the pie taste sour.
I forgot to boil the water, and so couldn't drain the mix,
Then the whole lot went quite solid, which left me in a fix.

The lard got almost everywhere, the mixture swelled up quick,
And like magic as I stirred it, the pie got ultra thick.
In a state of utter panic, with the situation grave,
I turned off the oven setting, and put on the microwave.
In ten minutes it was over, thank God I had my wish,
But the pie had now gone soggy, and turned into an ugly dish.

So it went back in the oven, with cheese upon the top,
To change its very nature, and become a total flop.
When my husband duly came from work, expecting fish or ham,
He tasted one small mouthful, to say 'By gum . . . it's lamb!'
He ate the pie with relish, then pain shot through his head,
For he slipped upon the egg I dropped, and landed up in bed.

Stan Mason

THE CAKE SHOP

Like painted silk
the cakes are there
for all to see
shall we buy some more for tea?
Nodding heads
in great unison
mouth-watering items
they can be.
But come December
will the shop be bare
the cakes have flown
do we care?
Sadness befalls us
in our tracks
we cannot see
the end in sight
but granted this
we still will strive
with all our might
to fill the shelves
into the night.

Joan Hands

IN A STEW

I love to cook
Do everything by the book
But sometimes it seems to be
Nothing turns out for me.
My cakes have dips and look like bowls
Sometimes have great big holes
My quiches are so flat
Look like cow pat.
If by chance I cook a fish
And hope it will be a tasty dish,
I put it in a lovely sauce
Still looks like it's swimming a river course.
No matter what I try to do
Between me and you -
I'm bound to end up in the stew.

Diane Norman

PEDAL BIN LOVE

The pedal bin looks attractive
In the corner
Of the kitchen.
I sidle towards its
Greyish hues,
And with right foot
Tentatively poised
I await the simple pleasure
It supplies;

The foot squeezes
Gently -
The lid rises
With a satisfying
Boing!
And stands there,
Strong and proud,
As a soldier
Stands to attention.

'That's good,' I think,
So I do it again -
So smoothly
The mechanism glides;
Several times in quick
Succession.
I glow and beam
With obvious delight
And wonder what,
In the scheme of things,
This strange pleasure of mine
actually means.

Christine McNaught

THE WORLD'S WORST COOK

Many times I've tried to bake
A soufflé or a flan,
But every time they seem to fail
- Or stick inside the pan!
Many times I've tried my hand
At classic *haut cuisine*,
It ends up in the doggy's dish
- And even *he* ain't keen!
Many times I've tried to make
A pastry or a dough,
They always seem to flake or stick
- Or shrink, or overflow!
My *victims* try these *delicacies*
But always feel *malade,*
- Thus if you can't smell burning,
It's sure to be sa-lad!

Esther Shaw

BETTY'S YORKSHIRE PUDDING

They all make fun at Betty's
poor excuse for Yorkshire pud,
it really is a standing joke
you'd ignore if you could.
The batter rises like a heavy mist
and this it is no lie,
but the recipe's top secret
so the pudding you must try.

Since the day of her experiment
her gruesome batter rises,
now her Yorkshire puds come in
assorted shapes and sizes.
These puddings now half fill the plates
Less room for meat and veg,
we simply pour the gravy on
the all-consuming wedge.
The size is so enormous
how do you stop it growing,
will it just engulf us all
we have no way of knowing.
This batter has to be one off
and I'd ban it if I could,
but no-one's ever found the recipe
for Betty's Yorkshire pud.

Margaret Johnston

THE PRESSURE COOKER

As my cooking is so mundane because of lack of time,
I bought a pressure cooker hoping to do the job just fine.
All went well for stews and soups, the family all ate well.
Although when served up day after day their faces rather fell.
I racked my brains to conjure up a new dish to prepare,
Then decided I would cook some rice to give them Indian fare.
The ingredients should be measured but I could not find my specs.
I threw the whole lot in the pan and muttered 'What the heck.'
Eventually the cooker hissed and then it hissed some more.
A large explosion sounded and it landed on the floor.
My husband rushed upon the scene to see what was amiss,
Just as the rice and peas and sweetcorn from the ceiling came adrift.
The poor man he was covered from head to toe in goo,
Needless to say the family meals have reverted back to stew!

Barbara Liles

A FRACAS AND A FISH SLICE

'I don't like them!'
'Oh, but Neighbours has begun!'
And, 'Urgh, not them again!'

These phrases are familiar
to mums across the land,
who think their lives would ease
if meal times could be banned.

As complaints arose one meal time,
mum retorted back
that no-one ever offers to help,
but still we give her flack.

She threw the fish slice into the sink,
meaning nothing else should be said.
Unfortunately it rebounded off the base of a pan
and belted my mum on the head.

Witnessed by my sister and I,
our laughs we desperately tried to hide.
While dad remained stolid as ever
waiting for the hoo-ha to subside.

It doesn't do to laugh
when your mother's in a mood,
but we learnt she was secretly laughing too,
but hid it to make the point to her brood.

Pamela Sibbering

DIET CAKE

A wet and rainy day
Not much to do today
Perhaps bake a cake?
'I'm on a diet!'
I'll make it for the family
That'll keep 'em quiet.

All that sugar and fattening butter
Makes my cake look nothing like humble
'It's for the family ' - I remind myself
As my tummy starts to rumble.

The wait seems long as the smell gets strong
So I decide to 'keep fit'
By doing an 'Aerobic' routine
To the latest No. 1 hit.

Really working hard, arms up and around
The aroma is strong now as I cool down
Feeling good and wide awake
I jog to the oven to view my cake.

Something's wrong! As I look through the door
It hasn't risen - not like before!
All that huffin' and puffin' with arms abound
Had knocked the oven dial around
It now read 'Grill on'
I couldn't believe it - all that hard work gone!

'Yoghurts for pud' I say as we sit down to tea
'They're so much better for you,' I smile sneakily.'

Wendi Hudson

KITCHEN CAPERS

We're giving our first dinner party tonight,
To celebrate the purchase of our first home,
The excitement is so intense,
The guests will soon arrive.

I've been made head chef tonight,
To feed and nourish the clan,
The food I have prepared,
I hope will be enjoyed by all.

The oven is so hot,
The chicken I'll soon place,
The tatties I'll boil,
The veg I'll do as well.

The meal is nearly ready,
Their places the guests do take,
To await the arrival of their meal,
That I have prepared.

The chicken to the table I do bring,
So proudly, start to carve,
The stuffing I do remove,
And nicely put upon a plate.

When asked 'What is that?'
'It's stuffing!' I proudly boast,
'Oh no it's not!' replies the wife,
As the guests begin to turn pale.

'Well what do you think it is?' says I,
'It's the giblets' she replies,
'I thought it was stuffing!' I replied,
Oh what a disaster to our first dinner party night.

Colin Forsythe

LIFE'S A CHEF

A chef I used to be at that. Food fights
Just too far to mention.
Kitchen capers you want to
Know. Through thick black smoke we all worked
On. Through sweat and tear right to the end.
Breakfast starts too early for me, try to
Cook breakfast with a hell's hangover, now that's a
Task I can tell you. As guests wait in vain for
Bacon 'n' eggs.
What's that smell? Toast-a-burning.
Black as hell! Oh what the hell, blame the waiter
As always we do.
Breakfast done, thank god for that. Eggs
On the floor, oh what a bloomin' mess.
Dinner comes too quick for me.
Pots-n-pans, what a bang, order this - 'n' - order that.
One pair of hands, that's all I've got. Throw in this,
Mix in that. That's what it's all about you know.
What was that, did someone shout,
Food fight? 'Splat' it's all ago, one death by chocolate
Cake flies swiftly through the air. Where it lands know
One knows, but what a mess.
In the end it's all a game, in
The life of a chef, I once used to be.

Craig Alan Hornby

HELL IN A HOT KITCHEN

Competitions can be fun
And here I am enjoying one
And stimulated to express
A culinary awful mess
I made of one.

A Sunday paper of renown
Offered a prize if we wrote down
A way to make an oyster dish.
Imagination fired my wish
To win the prize.

A telegram appeared one day
We like your recipe they say
You (and there's another two)
Come to display what you can do
To win the prize

Artichokes, the Jerusalem kind
And cream and sorrel (hard to find)
Tomato puree, just a little
Oysters to pile in the middle
To crown the dish.

The huge kitchen, hot as hell
Did not suit my dish too well
The handsome crown descended
Peaked cream became unblended
And slithered down.

The sorrel ringed the awful mess
A daisy dead it looked no less
Mortified I tried to ditch it
But adjudicators found it fit to have a prize.

I nearly died!

Vie Tulloch

BITTER BATTER PANCAKE

Today is Shrove Tuesday,
I am full of delight,
Forget those greasy burgers;
For it is pancakes for me for tea tonight.

With a plentiful supply of ingredients,
Mam weighed out every gram,
A display of savoury fillings;
And sweetened ones like jam.

As she poured out the mixture in the pan,
It turned darkish blue and lank,
And when it started blowing bubbles;
Her heart it almost sank.

For little Jimmy mistook sea salt,
For an opened box of soap powder,
And as it bubbled on and on;
The hissing got louder and louder.

Alas the pancakes were not edible,
But we had the cleanest ones in our street,
For they were almost whiter than white;
And sparkled like two washed feet.

But Mam she had a forgiving heart,
And laughed through her misery,
Then off she trots down to the shops;
To fetch fish and chips for tea!

Marina Elizabeth Siddell

TOAST

It's amazing what one can put on toast,
Besides butter, marmalade, or jam,
Just a simple task of toasting bread,
Bacon or eggs, or beans,
Cheese, tomatoes, or sardines,
The secret is hot toast, lovely golden brown,
No scraping off burnt black specks,
And turning the slices upside down,
Just a simple task of toasting bread.

Don't leave the kitchen or the toast will burn black,
Don't look for the postman, don't turn your back,
It's when the milk for the coffee is slowly on the boil -
The steam from the kettle fills the kitchen, fills the hall,
Then the toast needs turning or else it will spoil,
Just a simple task of toasting bread.

So every single morning up and down our street,
Can be heard the sounds of scraping coming
From houses smart and neat,
And it's not the sound of scraping coming
From muddy feet,
No! It's the scraping of the toast
Just a bit burnt around the edges,
It's such a simple task toasting bread.
'Mind the toast quick, quick mind the toast.'
'Mum. Isn't it time we got an electric toaster?'

Betty Eileen Houghland

PUPPY DOG CAPERS

I've got a new puppy he's one year old,
And for his age he's very bold,
Three slices of ham I put on a plate last night,
When I put the chips on they were nowhere in sight,
But who sat guiltily by the kitchen door,
My naughty puppy licking his paws.

And what do you think he then did,
Without warning he went and hid,
Where's that cheese gone from the table,
The wrapper left on the side with its label,
Oh you are a very naughty dog,
You should of been a wart hog.

A casserole with dumpling we'll have today,
Everyone shouts 'Hip hip hooray,'
Dumplings made and rolled into six balls,
Placed on a plate by the kitchen wall,
Hey three are missing six there were I'm not wrong,
Puppy, they were there but now they've gone.

He's always looking for grub to eat,
That's why he has big elephant feet,
He pinches any food he can get,
But he's a lovely dog, a brilliant pet,
A human dustbin that's what he is,
Food has to be hidden or he thinks it's his.

When in the kitchen you can hear me shout,
'Someone come and get this dog out,'
He looks at you with those sad eyes,
It really makes you want to cry,
With him about it's definitely Kitchen Capers,
Well that's it from me, I'm off to read my evening paper.

Ali Ashley

ON THE DEMISE OF A FAVOURITE PAN

In our youth, we were for ever gay,
    Afraid of nothing that came our way.
From breakfast eggs to Christmas feast -
    Creations, all, to say the least.
You've long out-lived your guarantee,
    Dare say the same applies to me!
We've done so much with merry heart.
    Now, alas, you've come apart.
You've lost your handle - I must 'get rid'.
    All that remains is your shiny lid.
Am I forgiven for advantages taken?
    I've burned your bottom - you've saved my bacon.
Together, we've accomplished much.
    Now you're a paintpot for my Old Dutch.

Joy M Tudberry

HOT CHILLI

As soon as I get in the kitchen,
I really get in a stew:
Cats, climbing onto the microwave:
And *that's* without mentioning you!
You clutter up my kitchen,
With hammers, drills and nails;
Spend half of my time avoiding
Tins of paint and freezing gales:
As you leave the back door open
While you just 'pop down the shed':
By the look of my Yorkshire pudding
When you come back in: you're dead!
Planks of wood, laid out on my worktop,
Doors, in front of the pedal bin;
And right in the middle, the cat is sprawled
Eyeing up the meat meant for the oven!
You tell me that soon you'll be finished
And then I will have what I'm missing.
That's great! Think I'll just count slowly to ten:
And picture my brand new kitchen!

Martina Peters

HANDY HINTS ON CLEANING THE COOKER

First gather tools which may be of use before your fingers get sore,
Just be assured when you're starting work there's nobody at the door,
Then smear the worst parts with any goo the adverts on TV praise,
It won't help much but makes you feel you're into a working phase.
Make sure you won't need a meal or drink and no one will visit you,
Then go away for a longish time, that goes for the family too.
Next cover surfaces round about with newspapers scattered free,
Including floor space where you might walk and anything you can see.
If rubber gloves aren't there to your hand reverse all you've done so far,
Bring everything back to normal quick and visit your local Spar.
Rub really hard with the nylon pad the demo man sold to you,
Remember he had a hidden strength, it's harder for me and you.
When you have finished this dirty job - and it's nearly finished you -
Then wash such tools as remain intact, the toothbrushes, nail files too.
Now scrape all newspapers from the floor and don't waste valuable time,
The mirror writing that's left behind cannot be classed as prime.
Flood all the floor with hot soapsuds and leave for a while to soak
And if you're one of the naughty ones now's the time for a smoke.
When seeing signs that the skirting boards are leaving their main support
It's time to mop up the surplus left and hope there's no damage wrought
(I have a penthouse so, praise be, all the tenants who live below
Give warning when it's time to dry that grubby invasive flow)
The lino probably will be lost, put that on your list to buy,
And add the paper that backs the sink, you'll never get this part dry.
Just one more thing to be tidied up, throw overalls firmly out,
You can try washing the rubber gloves and leave them lying about,
And then you can test if the fingers stick, if they do they'll have to go
I don't think you'll be satisfied that the job is a good one though,
And if you write to the firm to say that cleaning their stove's a chore
They'll tell you that model's out of date and ask how you managed before.

Joyce M Nicholson

I'M NO COOK!

I'm not all that good at cooking
Maybe I have never really tried
I find boiling potatoes quite easy
Or chips if you like them fried

I used to experiment in the kitchen
But nothing ever turned out as it should
I tried baking a potato in its jacket
And ended up with a half baked spud

I was given a recipe for a sauce mix
And in the pan it looked creamy and wet
But when it was poured over the dinner
The darned sauce curdled and set

Now you can't please everyone, sat at the table
But we all try to do our level best
Someone said that they didn't like rabbit
So I told them it was chicken breast

Now I can make a pretty good omelette
And toss it like a pancake through the air
Unfortunately I'm not the very best of catchers
And sometimes my pan isn't quite there

I've tried my hand at making a curry
And thrown most everything into the pot
But when I've sat down to my dinner
I found I'd made it too blooming hot

The worst thing for me in the kitchen
Is to study the recipe book
Because after I've finished my creation
It tells me I can't flipping well cook!

Thomas I Graham

KITCHEN CAPERS

To be a good cook is not in my line
Things never go right, they're wrong all the time
Take for example Shrove Tuesday to date
The kids wanted pancakes so they had to wait
'Til I'd mixed up the batter with beaten up egg
But I tipped up the basin spilling it down on my leg.

What was left over I fried in a pan
'Til one side was black and the other side wan
Then they had to be tossed, but oh! Dearie me
The kids laughed and laughed with hysterical glee
As one landed behind me and stuck to the door
The next one just lay there so limp on the floor

We scooped up the pieces and washed up the pan
No pancakes today we'll have toast and jam
That can't go wrong surely, my mind's in a whirl
But the toast in the toaster's beginning to curl
The bread was so thin it turned into crumbs
Oh! Get out the butter and butter some buns

We'll hot the buns up in the microwave now
They're shop ones of course, and I'll show you how
So much easier it is than making your own
Whoops! I've done it again, they're as hard as a bone
I left them too long, oh! 'Tis always the same
I won't make a cook - you can say that again.

Eileen Chamberlain

IT'S BOILED EGGS FROM NOW ON

I'm not what you might call the greatest of cooks
My efforts are mostly disasters
And when I'm let loose with a paring knife
My fingers all end up in plasters.

But once I assembled a salad complete
On this triumph my memory lingers
I did a great job and all that it cost
Were the tips of my two little fingers.

Now having got so far, I thought I'd surprise
My darling by making the dressing
So I got out the oil and the vinegar too
Plus a cookbook, I'm finished with guessing.

I got out the jar my wife kept just for shaking
The dressing into an emulsion
I filled it right up with some nice olive oil
And then I was filled with revulsion.

There's no room for the vinegar, some must go back
So I poured some oil back in the bottle
Now that was an error, the neck was too small
And it fell to the floor at full throttle.

I was sopping it up with a tea towel or two
When my wife came and started to roar
She made a mad dash with hands ready to clutch
And slid the whole length of the floor.

I guess I'll not try to do cooking again
I'm not cut out for this cooking biz
Now you'll have to excuse me, I must see my wife
And find out from the Doc how she is.

Joe Silver

LOOKING BACK

I look at the table
So firm and strong
Family all gathered
Were we belong
Many a meal
A strong decision took place
When our children were small
Decisions to make
That old table has known family fun
Ladened with jellies, birthday cake
Iced bun
As I recall once more
The sound of laughter
As games were played and won
Now the years have flown
Memories are all I have
Gone are those childhood days
Never to return
Just an ache in one mother's heart
Of things that might have been.

Irene Pearce

CORDON BLEU

When I am in my kitchen
with ingredients spread around.
I work hard at my cooking,
try new recipes I have found.

My aunt gave me the secret
of her 'never-fail' gingerbread.
I mixed it with the greatest care,
but it failed my family said.

I try so hard to boil some eggs,
but they're either hard or runny,
so we have to use a pick, or else
we spread those eggs like honey.

My Yorkshire puddings are a mess,
in fact, they're a disaster.
My roast potatoes always taste
like lumps of alabaster.

When I put vegetables in a pan
I cook them far too long.
I forget the time I lit the gas,
'til I smell a burning pong.

My salads are the only thing
that taste the way food should,
but can anyone go wrong with a salad?
Well yes, I suppose *I* could.

I think that if I wed again
he will *have* to be a cook,
then I'll just write my poetry
and burn my cookery book!

Daphne Richards

MY £10 WAGER

I'm not the greatest cook, there's been.
But on my day, I am quite keen.
One day I tried to make a cake,
A £10 wager was at stake.
So donned, with apron, eggs, and flour,
I hit the kitchen, on the hour.
I mixed, I baked, the hours passed.
My cake was ready, at long last.
Upon the plate, it looked a treat,
The time had come, for us to eat.
My friend, and I, picked up, and chewed,
We ate a little, but then we spewed.
You see, I'd made one tiny fault,
Instead of sugar, I'd used salt.
But to my friend, that fault was major,
And on those grounds, he won our wager.

Christopher A J Evans

FOOD TALKS!
(For all those who are calorie enhanced)

I'm a juicy red tomato, in the fridge, up the back
I yell out loudly '*Eat me*'
But I'm left a couple of weeks, through lack of interest,
And turn all black.

I'm a lovely orange carrot yelling *'Eat me, eat me up'*
I get grated into little pieces,
And just remain in the corner of the fridge,
In a cup.

I'm a round, red apple,
Healthy as can be
I scream loudly *'Eat me'*
You don't even hear me.

Yes all us fruit and vegies,
We can scream and yell all we like,
You just put us in the compost
And the worms eat us at night.

But I'm a packet of chocolate biscuits,
Sitting on the sink,
I hardly have time to whisper *'Eat me'*
And I'm gone in a flash, with a hot drink.

Robyn Jacob

SALAD DAYS

The lettuce in the salad bowl
Was a forlorn little thing.
She couldn't do aerobics,
Nor could she dance and sing!
While the vegetables around her
Were round and plump and green,
The lettuce was so limp and lost,
She hardly could be seen!
But, a tomato behind the pepper
Saw the lettuce's little head
And exactly one hour later,
(With lots of guests),
The loving pair were wed!

Moira Brabender

HOME MADE? . . .

Thought I'd take the plunge
And make a sponge.
Came out like a biscuit.
Didn't dare risk it
Again

. . . Till when
In-laws came for tea -
And, between you and me
His Mum's sponges are light -
Every mouth-watering bite
Makes one's senses delight . . .

Beat the marge and the sugar;
Beat the eggs, mixed the flour,
Stood and whisked just like crazy
For well over an hour . . .

The result of my toil
I wrapped up in foil
Deposited it in
My new swing-lid bin -

Another sponge no higher than
A pancake in the frying pan.

But . . .

All turned out well -
Though I can't hack it.

Thank goodness for
Cakes from a packet.

Dorinda MacDowell

MY KITCHEN

My kitchen is in light green
It's restful to the eyes.
The pot plants in the window
Are all just right for size.

Some of the tiles have pictures
Of tea and coffee pots.
The vinyl floor is soft brown.
The curtains have brown spots.

The cupboards hold my treasures
My boxes, tins and jars
So that in snowy weather
There'll be no need for cars.

My brand new dinner service
Has roses round the rims.
The cupboard next door to it
Has dusters, jifs and vims.

The polish made of beeswax
Makes furniture all shine.
The feather duster's useful
And sprays that smell of pine.

The vases are so pretty
From friends both near and far.
They fit in with the decor;
Look better than a jar.

My kitchen is a haven
It's peaceful all the time.
There I retreat from parties
And so it suits me fine.

Joyce M Turner

WHERE THERE'S A WILL

Prepare the meal well in advance was my instant theory.
But the meat has gone decidedly tough and the veggies all look dreary.
Out with the mincer, the masher too.
Carefully hiding it all from view.
Mix it all up, add a dumpling or two.
Instead of the roast, I got 'Thanks for the stew!'

Edith West

UNDER PRESSURE

It's clean and most efficient
and decidedly cuts time,
it cooks beef casserole beautifully
whilst you enjoy your wine.

Veg' and meat were nicely diced
so I put them in the pan.
As the hissing noise became a roar
I took my wine and ran!

I heard the slight explosion
as I quivered at the gate
'Pressure cooking is so safe'
or so the leaflet states.

All cooked now to perfection -
the aroma said it all
and it really looked delicious . . .
. . . as it slithered down the wall!

Vanessa Hulme

FIRST CLASS SERVICE!

We had a really good time last night,
We graced the table and looked so good,
The guests saw we were from the top drawer,
We knew just what to do with the food.

I've never seen the cook so wound up,
Her face so red and her temper sore,
Specially when dropping the frying pan,
And mushrooms flew all over the floor!

Things got worse when the cat joined the scene,
He thought something nice for him to eat,
But to his cost quite soon he found out
That mushrooms were not his kind of treat!

Whatever they had to eat that night,
There were no mushrooms to grace their plates,
Not enough time to go out for more,
In the panic they'd left it too late.

My blades were polished, your prongs were cleaned,
We lay there with the best china set,
Best tablecloth and expensive food,
Products of a hard day's toil and sweat.

What fun it was with you on the plate,
You holding the food for me to slice,
And when she'd finished and put us down,
Side by side she laid us, that was nice!

We couldn't wait to get in the sink,
When at last the guests had been well fed,
To have a good wash, be drained and dried,
And then put back in the drawer to bed.

If I could, to us I'd raise a glass,
A knife and fork of the highest class!

Mary Care

HARD SELL

Good morning to you Madam!
Sorry, did I wake you up?
Well, do I have a deal for you,
you won't believe your luck!

With every fitted kitchen
(*now prepare to be amazed*),
this month's special offer is
a built-in microwave!

You've never seen a microwave!
My dear where have you been?
They cook your food in record time,
they're every woman's dream.

And how about a freezer?
I can see you have the space.
Underneath the worktop seems to be
the ideal place.

You don't know what a freezer is!
I can't believe my ears.
How long were you asleep my love,
about a hundred years!

This really is a super deal.
Free fitting?
Absolutely!
Just sign along the dotted line.

Is that *Mrs* Sleeping Beauty?

Loraine Darcy

WHAT SHALL WE GIVE THEM?

The phone has rung; 'I'm dropping in -
Bringing with me Bill and Jim -
It's probable Julie will be there, if she's
Had time to dry her hair. We thought
We would arrive by one - just for a
Cuppa - biscuit - bun?'

'Golly gosh,' the clock says ten
No time to drive and shop with ease,
Besides, the purse looks very thin -
How much is left in that bread bin?
There's flour, basil a bit of cheese - and
Savoury scones filled to the brim.'

There's pasta lurking on that shelf
A carrot, onion, anything else? Oh!
Some potatoes large and bare - in
their skins they can go - in an
oven warm and low, topped with
parsley - they'll give a glow.

Three rashers will give that final touch
Stir fry the lot - it won't be much!
I've got some stock, curry powder too
Paprika, salt - I know what I'll do
A sauce I'll make to cover all.
There's garlic hanging on the wall.

'Come right in, this is simply great -
I *do* hope you'll have time to wait -
Stop for lunch, it won't take a tick
There's pasta, sauce and celery stick;
Hot, and herby cheesy scones
And potatoes with their jackets on!'

Joan Richardson

THE POTATO

Though epicures ever may try to attain
With fancy dishes aplenty
Endeavour to please and win the acclaim
By tickling the tastebuds of gentry
With soufflés and coolets and kangaroo goolies
Washed down with Chablis or hops
With barbecued snakes and crocodile steaks
And marinade oven pork chops
For afters there's rice with custard and spice
Of biscuits you just take your pick
Some other desserts you may find are quite nice
Like currants and sponge spotted dick
But there's naught to compare for versatile flair
You may mix it with cream and then whip it
You may roast it or bake it
But never forsake it
You can cut it in slices and chip it
Mash it or fry it however you try it
It's the one veg that's never a dud
For honour and fame it's won world acclaim
The common or plain garden spud!

Michael Cullen

COOKING FOR SUNNY JIM

My son you understand, is really very sweet
Except at reaching forty, he will hardly ever eat.
The problem really started when at the age of three
He had a dreadful illness which has put him all at sea.

I cook him cottage pie, sausage fry,
No, he will not even try.
Bowl of soup, he wouldn't stoop
Perhaps he'll eat a nice lamb roast,
Baked potatoes likes the most
Have some poached eggs on some toast,
Leave the eggs, bread upper most.

Let me mention cheese baked cod
Fancy I can see him nod,
I'll cook you plaice, or fillet kippers
He says 'One more and I'll have flippers.'
Ice-cream always seems a dream, also jam with clotted cream.
Never vegetables root or leaf,
Now he is frightened of the beef.

Of food, I know there's plenty more
Just want to take you on this tour
You know the slogan 'Peace not War'
I know, forced feeding - tried before!
So thankful that my family
The other four, including me
Enjoy our food that each day brings
The exotic and the simple things.

My son is married now you see
From all these problems I am free
His wife can carry on the game
I fear his diet's just the same.

Pamela Gibson

KITCHEN CAPERS

Can I, at seventy stop getting the lunch?
Tea and supper too?
Can I sit for once in a world of my own
Where words take precedence over 'You know who'

Can I ignore this dog of mine?
Who demands her food on the dot
Can't I provide just some bread and cheese?
But no they want a lot

I write a few lines then run off again
To the stove where it bubbles and cooks
They sit slavering away till it's all on the plates
And I fidget to get back to my books

Once more to write in a world of my own
Where my words in wondrous array
Come alive and walk, away from the page
To a world that's light years away

Where there is humour, beauty, and overall peace
Where magical 'Merlin' resides
And 'Pegasus' gold wings upon his heels
Whom even I can ride

To high flung mountains, a'sparkle at the top
Over seas of shimmering blues
With pirates, treasure, and jewels agleam
And for me some crystal shoes

But I come back to earth with a nudge on my knee
Eyes looking up plaintively
Then bustle in the kitchen somebody calls
'Mum anything nice for tea?'

Why can't they have some bread and cheese?
That they cheerfully get themselves
And leave me enraptured once again
In a land of witches and elves

So must I do penance to these pots and pans?
A slave to the stove now I see
So it's farewell to 'Merlin' 'Pegasus' too
As it's nearly time for tea

Joan Eyles

A COOKERY BOOK NIGHTMARE

Have you ever noticed, that when you try to cook
It never comes out looking like the picture in the book
Once I tried a soufflé, it came out looking flat
I could have used it as a double for a front door mat
Then I tried a gateau, the picture looked so nice
It came out flat and lifeless so I left it for the mice
Next morning when I went to see, if the mice enjoyed their grub
Not only had they left it, they'd put it in a tub
Once I slaved for hours, trying to cook a roast
But when I gave it to my folks they said they liked my toast
I've tried to cook a rabbit but it looked more like a duck
And it came out looking blacker than the wheels upon a truck
I tried but once to add some fun and tried a new adventure
I made some toffee treacle cakes but Gramps just broke his dentures
The only things that I can cook, that don't come out a flop
Are the ones that in a microwave you only have to pop
I don't mind making sarnies and things of equal ease
But the only things I put inside are simple things like cheese
I don't know if it's only me who always seems to fail
I persevere and keep on trying, but alas to no avail!

Jane Kay

CAN COOK WON'T COOK

I tried my hand at curry
I'd never cooked before
I needed some hot spices
Then needed more and more
I sat down at the table
The plate it looked a treat
The curry tasted lovely
But forgot to add some meat
I've cooked bacon that spat at me,
I've had eggs refuse to boil
Their shells just split right open
I'd run out of cooking oil
The coffee pot spilled over
The water boiled away
A kitchen can be lethal
When you cook from day to day

Robert Price

MORE HASTE - LESS SPEED

I thought a Bramley apple I would bake
In my microwave, just two minutes it would take,
But when I looked
It was far from cooked,
So I gave it just two minutes more
And the horrid thing exploded round the door.
Although it was most tight enclosed,
The lid blew off and the juicy mess exposed
Itself before my unsuspecting eyes.
Truly an unexpected culinary surprise.
I rescued what I could
And as I finished up my pureed pud
I thought that next time I would give it three mins no more,
And open up most carefully the microwaving door.
The point about the microwave is its turn of speed.
But if you overdo it -
You certainly will rue it
And the mess it makes just overtakes
Hungry hopes of instant feed.
But despite my rueful groans about it
I certainly wouldn't be without it.
You've simply got to understand
The microwave requires a very gentle hand.

Eileen M Lodge

KITTEN CAPERS

What do you think you're doing?
Please get down from there.
The surface's not for playing on,
but, you don't really care.

What did you knock that down for?
Now you've made another mess.
I've got to clear it up now,
You are a rascal Tess.

The surface has got fur on,
it's white, just like yours.
Now, I've wiped it over,
Get down. Remove your paws.

Who's been in the fridge then?
The door is open wide.
The milk has got knocked over,
the cheese gone from inside.

Why do you look so guilty?
hanging on the curtain there.
I wanted to make pancakes,
with the cheese that isn't there.

L Gillard

KITCHEN DILEMMA

I tried my hand in the kitchen
To make a custard pie.
A nice clean dish to put it in,
I really felt quite high.

Lined the dish with short crust pastry,
Then did bake it blind.
It was my mother's recipe
So hoped it would be kind.

Getting egg mixture ready to put into the dish,
For success well, I could only wish.
Then into the oven to cook,
Daring not to take a look.

At last the pleasure had arrived
To show off the custard pie.
Into the oven then I dived
To show all that I really did try.

But alas disaster had struck,
The bottom of the pie had stuck
Itself right to the top and side,
Open up that big hole, so I can drop and hide.

Evelyn M Harding

CHRISTMAS DINNER

This special dinner once a year is a tasty treat,
Although for me it is nothing but a mammoth feat.
I never sleep well the night before,
Is it the thought of tales and folklore?
No it's the thought of turkey, Christmas pud and mince pies,
I rise at seven-thirty with tired weary eyes.
I grab the turkey thinking into the oven you go,
It won't be cooked fast, I'm doing it slow.
I look around and see a wonderful sight,
The vegetables are done, I did them last night.
Sausage rolls and mince pies are next on my list,
I hope there is nothing that I have missed.
After hours of slaving over a hot stove,
I look a right mess, my face has gone mauve,
But I don't mind as I look around with pleasure,
Everything looks great, surely a meal to treasure.

My husband's delight changes as he starts to carve
He shouts 'I'm not eating this I would rather starve,'
What's wrong, what's wrong?' demands my son,
I still did not know what I had not done.
The turkey had been cooked entirely whole,
Its giblets still buried deep into its soul,
One thing's for certain, I will argue no more,
Next year we go and dine with my mother-in-law.

Linda Turner

HOME MADE SOUP

I love the taste of loop-de-loop
That's good old fashioned home made soup
Pea and ham is a favourite of mine
It smells so yummy and tastes divine
So I went straight to work to make some today
And loaded the pressure cooker all the way
It hissed and bubbled merrily away
And I felt proud of my effort today
Feeling kind of tired and worn
I left the soup all on its own
And as I rested in the chair
I almost forgot the soup cooking there
When from the kitchen came a bang
A hiss a splutter a pop a twang
I gingerly peeped my head around the door
And never had I seen such a mess before
The peas were dripping from the light
And some were actually still in flight
Dripping down windows over ceiling and floor
Skidding and slipping right out of the door
I ducked and dodged my way through the mess
To try and salvage my new pink dress
With one final bang the whole thing exploded
Leaving me covered all over and feeling loaded,
Standing there looking forlornly around
Noting there wasn't a dry patch to be found
This is the end I cried as I wept
Walking out of the kitchen totally bereft
And from that unforgetful day
I only have soup when I am away.

Millicent Boal

U N BEATON

I have bought a new cook book,
So I think I'll take a look.
To practise all my culinary skills
With the trimmings and the frills.

Let's see . . . Beef Wellington . . . good grief!
I've plenty of Wellie, but alas no beef.
What about Spaghetti Bolognaise . . . ?
Dear me . . . no pasta . . . now I'm in a daze.

A dish from France, that's 'Coq au Vin'.
We will pretend that we're in Cannes.
The chicken legs have done a runner en-masse,
So that Vin has gone down the crevasse.

I'm running out of time . . . it's almost four.
I can hear my husband opening the door.
'Dear! You've made the meal I love the most!'
'Super, scrumptious, beans on toast!'

Anne Sharman

STEW AND DUMPLINGS

Who cares if I can't cook
What's there to know
You only follow this book
This is it I'll make a stew
I'll even make dumplings
Just to please you.
The mother-in-law's coming around her they flock
When she tastes this stew she'll be in for a shock.

She thinks I can't cook
I'll give her a surprise
It's going to be great
The best in their lives
I bought ingredients
The suet too
I piled in the veg
It looked just like glue
Oh well it smells OK
I just hope it tastes nice I cross fingers and pray

Table's set napkins are out
Bring the stew, she did shout
Everything looks lovely
Oh what a delight
But where were the dumplings
They were nowhere in sight
I put them in they'll be at the bottom
I never forget that stew it was rotten
I didn't know, flour I had to add
My dumplings dissolved
That's why it was so bad.

There was no wonder it looked like glue
Never again it was a horrible stew
My husband couldn't eat it and he's a hog
Everyone left it including the dog.

Margaret Newton

KITCHEN CAPERS

We were newly married, it was nearly Christmas time.
We were given some sweet chestnuts, they really looked quite fine.
We put them in the oven, then went out for a walk,
Our chestnuts soon would warm us, we thought they'd be sublime!

We came back to our smart kitchen, and opened the oven door -
Bang! Bang! Our chestnuts shot right out, all around the floor!
We gazed forlornly at the mess, with tears in our eyes of shock and mirth!
We realised what we had done wrong - we forgot to slit the chestnuts' girth!

We shook with helpless laughter, as we tried to tidy up,
So we put the shining kettle on, and had a big brew-up!
So instead of our hot chestnuts, a cuppa kept us warm.
There's nothing like a cup of tea, it helped to keep us calm!

Ruth L Daly

LAPSES

I'm standing alone in my pantry,
What have I come in here for?
It can't be the eggs or the sugar
I'd have thought of them before.

I wonder if its the spices?
Now what did I start to make?
Could it have been melting moments
Or a nice big fruity cake?

I'll retrace my steps to the kitchen
And look in the cookery book.
Perhaps it will help me remember
What it was I started to cook.

The flour and the salt's in the basin,
Now what else does it say that I need?
Of course! It's the fat that I'm wanting
Phew! I really am feeling relieved.

It seems that my memory is failing,
Brought on by old age they do say.
So I'll just have to try and remember
To write things down every day.

But, wait! There could be a problem!
I've suddenly thought it through,
I'll forget where I put pen and paper,
So I'm back to square one - 'help do!'

Vivienne Roberts

COMEDY OF ERRORS!

I used to wonder why my wife
Would suddenly be twitching
Each time I said I'd like to have
A work-out in the kitchen.

Well OK, so I might have dropped
Just one or two small clangers,
I've found out why the sausages
Are also known as bangers!

I just forgot to prick the things.
The pan I overloaded.
I only left them for a while
And everything exploded!

She wasn't well. Her scrambled egg
She wanted lightly toasted.
The saucepan turned a shade of black.
The bread I sort of roasted!

One night she said 'I'm going out,
Your dinner's there. Just heat it.'
I just don't know what I did wrong.
The dog refused to eat it!

I've grilled, I've fried, I've roasted too
I'm sure it should be easy.
Yet when I cook I always find
My stomach feels quite queasy!

In case you think it's all bad news,
In style I'll end this ballad.
Here's one that I made earlier.
Mind you, it was a salad!

John Christopher Cole

KITCHEN CHAOS

My date was arriving any minute
and I hadn't prepared any food,
out came a frozen lasagne
and a bottle of cheap booze,
I'd stick it in the microwave
and say I'd made it myself,
and pour him a glass of wine
and toast our very good health.

Hang on he's here now knocking
and the fuse in the plug has blown,
I'll have to get him to fix it,
but after saying 'bugger it',
he's stormed off home!

Claire Young

THE NON EPICURE

When Bill's wife was taken quite poorly, and
lay in her hospital bed,
She worried however he'd manage, and if he'd be
properly fed.

She gave him a list of instructions, on things
that she thought he should know!
He hadn't done very much cooking, but, he
promised her he'd have a go!

That night he was feeling quite peckish,
So he thought to himself, 'have a treat'
His taste buds were all of a tingle,
When he saw all the good things to eat!

There was bacon and eggs in the pantry,
Some tomatoes and cheese on the shelf!
Ingredients galore were piled up in the store,
To make something special himself!

The freezer was bursting with goodies,
There were burgers and pies by the score!
Sausage! Pizzas! And flans a selection of cans,
and a bottle of wine in the drawer!

When he looked at the feast laid before him,
He pondered which he fancied most!
Then he finished up grabbing a bottle of beer,
and making some baked beans on toast!

L Muscroft

PASTRY FOOLS

Have you ever had a pastry fight?
We did once at school.
The teacher had just left the room
So we thought we'd play the fool.

One Irish lass, a red head,
And always game for a laugh,
Was the first to start it -
She never did things by half.

All her shortcrust pastry
Was rolled into a ball.
First she threw it to me,
And then to one and all.

Now and then, it fell to the floor,
And gathered a bit more dirt.
But this did not bother us,
We'd just roll it down our skirts.

Suddenly the Irish lass
Hurled the ball towards the door,
Just as it was opening
To the footsteps of Miss Moore.

The pastry hit her in the face.
Gob smacked, you could say.
And we? Yes got detention
At the end of the day!

Diane Mary Watt

FISH EYES

A nice piece of mackerel I cooked for his tea
He looked on his plate, then he looked up at me.
I will always remember that puzzled look.
Then he said to me 'Darling do you know how to cook?'
I was feeling quite proud of myself before he said this to me.
Again he said 'Darling, this fish should not be looking at me'
I told him to put a blindfold over his eyes.
He laughed so much he had tears in his eyes,
Then he opened it up with the guts still inside
I will always remember that look of surprise
I should have gutted it and cut off his head.
But I washed it and grilled it instead
Placed on a plate with a slice of brown bread.
It was the first meal I cooked since we were wed
I now know I must gut it and cut off its head
The giggles that night as we laid in our bed
Now every time we have fish for our tea
I look at him, he looks at me
Then we burst out laughing hysterically

Maureen Ellen Williams

MY SWEET TOOTH

One weekend I recalled I quite liked to bake
Coffee meringues and rich cherry cake
On the top shelf alone lay my recipe book
Led by my sweet tooth I had a little look
Chocolate eclairs and egg custard pies
Pictures making my taste buds cry
Tying on the apron bringing out the flour
Starting with something simple that'll be ready in an hour
The cake's in the oven it's due out at three
I'm anticipating a slice with a nice cup of tea
Times up out it comes that cake looked nice
Smelling of ginger and a little spice
Now in my kitchen I have a tendency to dream
Things aren't always as good as they may seem
After the first bite disappointment took over
Was I so absurd not to have added any sugar
Drinking my tea with bread and jam on top
Next time cake takes my fancy I'll be out to the shop

Janet Lythe

TENDER MOMENTS

I'd like to tell you
What happened to me
One day while I was cooking
I suppose you could say
It served me right
Because I was not looking

I had made a lot
of banana fritters and
Some batter had stuck to the fork
What I did not know
That I would burn my lips
And would not be able to talk

My family did their best
By trying not to laugh
Told me that tea was very nice
But all that I could eat that night
Was an ice cube and a cucumber slice

Patricia Belfield

NO LA CARTE

I looked at my daughter's treacle tart
It really was a work of art
She gave me advice and the recipe
I was going to make one for my tea
I bought the ingredients from my local shop
Including cornflakes for the top
I went to the cupboard where my utensils are kept
I felt excited quite adept
I followed the recipe to the latter
Then my neighbour popped in for a chatter
So I put my tart in my microwave
Thinking of the time I would save
We chatted for ages on and on
I heard a bang something was wrong
My microwave door hung on its hinges
My treacle tart a mass of cinders
I had treacle running down my door
Bits of pastry on my floor
My neighbour looked at my face in despair
She didn't laugh, she didn't dare
It was easy to get it off my floor
A little harder off the door
But now I must decorate after all
For as I scrubbed paper came off the wall
My daughter phoned asking 'How was your tart'
Well put it this way, 'I'm no la carte'.

Barbara Ramsey

COOK'S LAMENT

To me the kitchen is a minefield,
Danger in every step I take;
The fire brigade is sent for,
Whenever I start to bake.

I specialise with beans on toast,
The type of high class food I like the most;
A change of menu usually means,
Something different, like toast on beans

When they rebuild my burnt out kitchen,
Then a new cooker I will but;
It wasn't really my fault,
When the old one was blown sky high.

My home is now a war zone,
And I'm left here to dine alone,
Not a morsel left in the house,
Now, where did old Fido hide his bone?

Ronald Duck

SAUSAGE CALYPSO

Encased in its skin, some are lovely and thin
And the taste is so pure and so clear
Some others are fat - no doubt about that
An institution that we hold dear

The flavours are full, we can sit and can mull
Which taste we favour each day
To put in our pan, to eat while we can
To the world we show the way

The sausage is found to be very sound
In every house, castle or inn
The sound that it makes, beats making cakes
To grill to perfection's no sin

But when I try, a sausage to fry
There's quite a system or knack
'Cos one side is done - the other's no fun
Oh no - this sausage is black

A sausage to prick - will that do the trick
To make it a rich golden brown
My mother came in, said 'That's quite a sin'
(I noticed she wore a dark frown)

Not even the dog, will eat this burnt log
I'll have to throw it away
It's not such a joke - I can't see for smoke
This happens to me every day.

Mary Hulme

THE YORKSHIRE PUDDING

I put in flour and then the eggs,
the milk and water to.
The dish is heating in the oven,
because this is what you do.
I've followed the book, and Mum's advice.
I just wish I could cook it, and cut a slice.
But instead, I end up with a gooey mess,
I followed instructions, more or less.
I try and I try, but just cannot do,
a Yorkshire pudding, Mum, as good as you.

Sandra Houghton

TAKING DRASTIC MEASURES

As if decimalisation wasn't enough
We now have to measure in kilos and stuff
Those people in Brussels, now make all the rules
To which we comply like subservient fools

Three-quarters of mince, has always been such
Convert it to grams, and it sounds far too much
Cooking was once creative and fun
A handful of this, and that, and it's done
But now that it's all got to be so precise
The shopping and measuring part's not so nice

Brussels can lay down whatever restriction
But I'll do what I please, thank you, in my own kitchen
Tomato puree and Worcester sauce
Will be measured in 'squirts' as a matter of course

Dry ingredients, like sugar and flour
Bicarb and salt, and baking powder
Will be measured in 'smidgens' 'handfuls' and 'piles'
And still produce cakes that are better by miles

Liquid measures can be also got round
By turning the bottle upside down
And counting the 'glugs' as they ooze from the neck
The quantity's always the same (you can check!)

While Brussels continue to rule in our stores
We can do what we like, behind closed doors
And Brussels may judge me to be a sinner
But I won't have their sprouts, on my Christmas dinner!

Margaret Sanderson

TRY AGAIN

I cannot ever make an omelette
How ever hard I try.
It always turns to scrambled egg
What is the reason why?

Amy Barrett

THAT SPECIAL MEAL

A special meal I thought I'd make
a bit of effort it did take.
A lovely joint of meat I'd bought
A new way I'll try, I thought.
The Yorkshire's rose, they were great
All going well, no running late.
Flushed and happy we sat down to eat
This I felt would be a treat.

After two mouthfuls, maybe three
My dearest looked and said to me
'I'm very sorry I can't eat more.'
My heart it sank down to the floor.
'No more dinner - I've had my fill.
I really do feel far too ill.'
Was I angry, cross or mad
Yes - but my hubby did look bad!

P M Low

RECIPE FOR DISASTER

I spend hours in the kitchen,
I try with all my might
But no matter what I do
It never turns out right.

I've tried my hand at everything
I'll always try my best
I just haven't got a clue
And that, I have confessed.

I've had such fun with my frying
I have tried to flambé,
And when I served up mussels, we
Were off for three days.

My deserts are a disaster,
My soufflés will not rise
For all my cooking efforts
I will not win a prize.

I really try my best to please
Ad what more can I do?
I'll make just one promise, I'll
Try not to poison you.

Jennifer Emery

THE FOOD OF LOVE

When I got married yesterday,
Nobody said I'd have to say,
I can't cook!

Recipes, cookbooks are a mystery,
I'd much rather watch TV,
I can't cook!

We're really hungry, what will we do,
None of us has got a clue,
'Cos we can't cook!

We'll get a Chinese carry out,
Tomorrow a kebab, it's better than nought,
We still can't cook!

The shiny kitchen is still brand new,
The meals cooked there are very few,
We still can't cook!

Who cares,
We share.

Elizabeth Loy

HOME IS WHERE THE FOOD IS

Peckish I was feeling
And so kitchen-ward I went
Eating was my mission
And on that I was hell bent
Something light to snack upon
With cooking time of not too long

Omelette was my first thought
But eggs were not what I craved
The pizza in the oven
Yeah, the one that I had saved
Unfortunately not I fear
For fur and flies did feature here

'Toast' I cried 'I've got it now
I almost feel I'm fed
Uh oh now wait a minute
Mmm, I think I'm out of bread
I'm outta here - I gotta dash
I'm back again - I'm outta cash

Saltfish, spinach, calaloo
That's really what I need
Home is where the family is
So that's where I'll find feed
'Dad, lend us a coupla pound
What's cooking Mum? I'm coming round'

Debbie Charles

A NOTABLE EVENT

My hubby was a churchman -
A man of God was he
One night a fellow curate
Came to our house for tea

We had a pleasant evening -
Then came the time to part
Both said they'd wash the dishes -
Such culinary art!

An hour passed - or maybe two
I wondered what had happened to
those godly men so fine and true.

I peered through the kitchen door -
before my startled gaze I saw
A scene I'd never seen before -

The dishes washed by curate one
were put aside - forgotten -
and washed again by curate two

So intent were they discussing
Deep thought in a higher plane
Enthralled in contemplation
Their work went down the drain

Ad infinitum I believe
Had I not happened on the scene

Glenys Thomas

THE FOOD FIGHT

The food fight was really very funny,
We were throwing chips and spoonfuls of honey!
The cookery teacher said we were very bold,
And to my friends and I she began to scold!
'How many times have I told you to be good?
And never play or throw your food?'
With heads hung low we stood there,
Looking at nothing but thin air.
The room was a great, big mess,
And I was really in distress!
What if my parents find out?
The worst I can get will be a clout.
We cleaned the room and washed the floor,
Then the brushes and mop were put back in the store.
The teacher then sent us to the headmaster,
And suddenly our fun was now a disaster!
I knocked on the master's door,
But found myself lying on the floor.
The nurse said I collapsed with fear,
But I'd put it down to the food fight beer!
All too clear I remember the food I threw,
Chips, beans and spoonfuls of stew!
That was all in the past,
And the food fight memory didn't last.
There has never been another fight in the past,
And I sure hope that one wasn't the last!

Louise Turner

COOKING FOR ONE

Cooking for one can be fun
There is no excuse, whatever folk say
To let the thought of it ruin your day
To make yourself a tasty treat
Can defeat a lonely feeling
Sending all your taste buds reeling
There is no end to what you can make
If you acquire the urge to bake
There are loads of recipes just for you
Cooking for one is nothing new
Of course, if you don't like eating alone
There *is* something that can be done
Invite a friend to share your meal
It is possible you could make a deal
The invite returned would give you a break
From making that meal for your own sake
Think about it! It can be done
You do not have to cook for one.

Evelyn A Evans

HELP

My wife is leaving me this morn,
In three more hours she'll be airborne;
So can I be a bachelor gay
In those six weeks whilst she's away?

I've never used this stove before
Or that machine beside the door:
How will I cook my broccoli green;
How will I get my best shirt clean?

I won't have time for bachelor games
With wine and song and painted up dames
I won't have time for very strong drink
When I have both my hands in the sink!

Oh, why do men get foolishly fond
Of wives who leave and quickly abscond?
Why do we yearn for their speedy return?
Because we don't like our dinner to burn.

Well really six weeks are not very long
To anyone who has willpower strong,
But I am a weakling with fast knocking knees
So come home soon, darling, *and hurry it please!*

Mervyn S Whale

PANCAKES

I looked up and there
It was
My pancake on the ceiling
After all the effort
Making it
It was an awful feeling

I tossed another in
the pan
Then I tossed once more
This one didn't make
The ceiling
But landed on the floor

I'll try once more and
hope this one
Lands upon my plate
Because my kitchen's
Looking
In a very sorry state

My third attempt success
At last
It seems I've passed
The test
Now I'll sample my pancake
And take a well earned rest

Edna M Jones

IN THE KITCHEN

The washing machine is on the blink,
Scrub the clothes in the sink,
The tumble dryer has had its day,
Back to the clothes ropes, and pray,
The dishwasher, what a puddle,
Really really what a muddle,
The kitchen sink is full again,
It's working overtime well then,
What is next, the electricity is gone,
Makes one feel, a bit forlorn,
What a day, what more to say,
Maybe tomorrow it will be okay.

Sheila MacDonald

THE EGG FROM HELL

This sad story that I do tell
About a man called Matt
And the egg from hell

He took it in a gentle grip
It slid straight of his finger tip

A sudden dive to save that egg
His foot it struck the table leg

A awful noise and dreadful din
The table fell on top of him

Milk and butter and jam galore
Splattered on the kitchen floor

He looked towards the open door
And saw the egg upon the floor

He tried to pick it up with care
And slipped right down the landing stair

At the bottom to his wife he said
Perhaps I'll have beans on toast instead

Matt Pearson

YORKSHIRE PUDDING BLUES

Yorkshire pudding blues.
Of what was I accused.
To impress my mate,
On this dinner date.

Puddings to start,
The way to his heart.
Ingredients beaten,
Now no worry.

But, all went wrong
and in a hurry.
New flour I'd used
In my creation.
Didn't bring the
expected elation.

Non-appealing,
Flat as pancakes
Heavy as steel.
My first disaster
of the culinary kind.
Ruined for life
What a bind.

In my case, just not so.
He put it down to nerves
Trying to impress,
To be all things
Be the best.

Now we're married,
All is well.
And yes, you've guessed
My puddings are swell.

Andrea Edwards

MY KITCHEN

The kitchen is the place to be
Especially on baking days with me,
I mix some scones at first you see
In case some friend calls for a cup of tea.

Then I make some nice short pastry,
Like a raspberry pie which is sweet and tasty,
Lemon meringue pie is what we like most
Also almond tarts with nuts browned like toast.

But best of all is fruit cake all moist
With a drop of the hard stuff which gives it a hoist,
I sometimes make flans with lots of fresh eggs
Mushrooms, chives, cheese and some veg.

My kitchen is not a modern fitted one
It's old like me just keeps pottering on,
Blue is the dominant colour of my doors
With lots of blue crockery on the walls.

My dining table is shining bright
With a bowl of flowers to my delight,
With visitors coming to my back door,
Next to the kitchen with lovely smells they adore.

Bessie Metcalfe

WHAT A PUD!

When I worked for seven years as a cook
On the garden suburb of London town
I had this unusual experience
Which I will now write for you down

I remembered a recipe one day
Which my mother had made years before
and we all of our own family
did this special pudding always adore

We will be very pleased to try it
said the mistress with a big smile
and I felt quite puffed up with pride
this made me so pleased all the while

To make my dear Mum's special pudding
was a tremendous occasion for me
and as I had praised it so very much
more important it truly was to be

A batter mixture with fruit in the middle
tied up in a special cooking cloth
then gently boiled in a pan of hot water
until it was cooked thorough enough

But as soon as I undid the string
what a sloppy mess flew everywhere
I had made a mistake with the recipe
and my heart was filled with utter despair

But the mistress she started to laugh
as the funny side she could then see
with this sudden cooking confusion
which was the new pudding or me.

Doris Middleditch

MAYONNAISE

Said the companion of her bed:
'One request - the very best
for my most important guest.
Don't overdress, put up your hair,
casual wear with mother's pearls;
my boss he likes the pretty girls.'

Table laid in the shade
beneath a tree, set for three
on damask cloth spotless white,
knives and forks polished bright.

But in the kitchen lurks disaster
the mayonnaise she cannot master,
beating, beating, ever faster,
hair in wisps, crimson face,
no credit to him, a disgrace.

Another yolk, another yolk . .
'til like the fragile shells she broke
took up the bowl and threw the whole
at the very special guest.

Such commotion no promotion
wife in mini skirt and jacket black
to work goes back, in kitchen never more
except to do some menial chore,
peel potatoes, just a few,
stir his version of her homely stew.

Friends come and sing his praise,
'To the cook,' their glasses raise,
her toast is to the best of days
when freedom came through mayonnaise.

Brigit Barlow

GET THE PICTURE

I have often wondered why my cooking never looks
Like example pictures in my glossy cookery books.
Shiny colour photographs of mouth-watering delights,
Are shown with sauces gleaming from photographer's flashlights,
With colour, texture (and no doubt, taste) all perfect in each way
While my reality is a mush in a suspicious shade of grey.
I've tried boiling, baking, frying, stewing,
Every time I'm sure I know exactly what I'm doing,
But never does my output match the item on the page,
If I wasn't such a calm one I would fly into a rage.
I'm fortunate that there's no need to throw it all away
For my husband always eats the lot and says it is OK.

Ann Hobbs

ALL IN A FLAP JACK

Oats, sugar, syrup and margarine
A simple recipe, so it would seem
Flapjacks were chosen, those I could master
A decision was made, and begun the disaster.

I measured the oats ounce by ounce
Unaware that my cat was ready to pounce
Then, I weighed sugar with very great care
But moggy then leapt and sent sugar in air.

As I swept sugar up from the floor
The cat's life was saved by a knock at the door
An animal lover stood shaking a tin
So I gave him a pound and forced him a grin.

In the oven at last for ten minutes precisely
Chocolate on top would go ever so nicely
I'd pop to the shop for five minutes at most
But delayed in the traffic, my cake burned like toast.

So, I opened the chocolate and sat on a chair
And the cat looked up with eyes of despair
I smiled and gave that forgiving look
It's not your fault that I was not born to cook.

Joyce Barclay

ETIQUETTE

I thought organic veg for a change
And corn-fed chicken, plump and free range.
Blow the expense I know we are able
To afford it, so setting a perfect table,
Prepared a sumptuous feast with ease,
Knowing I would be sure to please
I got everything right I thought and yet,
I wiped my nose on my serviette
 - Not etiquette

J Facchini

KITCHEN CAPERS

What shall I cook for the family today I think I'll try
something new,
An oriental dish perhaps, a change from the steak or stew.
I've gathered the ingredients all together the veg are washed,
and chopped.
At last the dish is filled it looks so nice, and into the oven it's popped.

I settle down to a cup of tea, put my feet up on a stool,
Then an awful thought fills me head oh no I cry you fool.
I rush to open the oven door and there to confirm my fears
Lay the dog's dish with his dinner inside, I suddenly burst into tears.

No time now to cook that different meal, my husband arrived - what a pity,
But his words were like music to my ear, 'Let's dine out tonight in the city.'

Ruth Lyttle

KITCHEN CAPERS!

We were marvellous together
Between that table and the stove
Making jars and jars of marmalade
Which our friends indeed did love!

We weighed the sugar carefully,
And matched the water to the fruit,
Sometimes it gelled successfully,
Sometimes it left us mute!

How wonderful were those fruit cakes
As for weeks and weeks on end
We made those tasty morsels
To share with many a friend!

And then disaster struck at us
As you drove me to despair,
Refusing to trust my weighing
Of the ingredients standing there!

You complained about the sugar;
You complained about the fruit;
You mistrusted all my measuring;
You treated me like a brute!

No more fruit cakes for ever!
But then you were the boss
Who would never be convinced,
So your husband bore the cross!

Then came the old hen's party
On each Thursday afternoon-
Macaroons and rock cakes
And tea, served by this buffoon!

Now twenty years later I wish you were here -
We'd make another fruit cake, just for us, my dear!

Claude Knight

THE BATTENBURG MUTINY

I sneak away, a coward with stealth,
to find peace with quiet, and good health,
for today, it's special, a cake has to bake.
A frenzy of arguments and, 'for heaven's sake.'

I find it much better to be stretched out with a book,
than to be laid out with a rolling pin's 'left hook',
for ingredients of pastry and me, disagree,
a glutinous mess, there is surely to be.

Why is it women, pick on the worst moments,
to decide and to do jobs, without much portents, and omens,
The family divide, to all points of the compass,
hopefully wishing, their absence, does not, detract us.

Alan Noble

THE MENU

Folks are coming to stay for the day,
Menu to be thought out without delay.
Shall it be something hot or cold,
Indecision sets in, oh come on be bold.

Why of course a recipe not tried before,
Perhaps not, they may decline to ask for more.
Handkerchiefs will come out to hide the blessed 'burps,'
'Cause high in the duodenum a lump of food still lurks.

Too many bones, it can't be fish,
Or a delicious meat pie, a favourite dish.
Though if arriving full of apologies an hour late,
A pie crust turned to leather, now! I must debate.

How about a good hot curry, oh, the mind boggles,
One visually sees them rushing out with the 'colly-wobbles.'
Yet, the humble ploughman's may be a winner,
But they will secretly think, oh what a small dinner.

What for 'sweet' Charlottes, trifle or flan of mince,
No! They'll think about their figures and quietly wince.
A cool sweet melon would go down well,
Tentatively my apple pie I'd try to sell.

Oh dear, somehow I'm not feeling too well,
It's these hot sweats that give me hell.
I'm at a funny age you see dear,
'Hot' from top to toe dear,
No! No! They must come next year.

Queenie Marshall

THE KITCHEN

I met my friend one summer's day,
She invited me round for tea.
And after a quick look in the door,
It seemed rather amazing to me.

She beckoned me into the kitchen,
The curtains, hung upside down.
The teapot, minus its lid on the stove,
And crockery thrown all around.

The bin was old and messy,
An old tattered mat by the door.
I took a peep at the light shade,
Dirty as well, was there more?

On the wall was an old broken mirror,
A string of dried onions as well.
It was home to her pets I'm sure of that,
And part of her life you could tell!

Edith Blissett

THE DIETER

That fridge is too inviting as I creep across the floor,
Though I have to shut my eyes 'cos' my diet's on the door.
Behind that door sat on a plate -
A cake so creamy
'I just can't wait!'

But no - hang on I must be strong,
Just one look - 'No No' it's wrong.
I've done so well I can't give in,
Oh God, why didn't you make me thin?

I'll have a little bite or just a little pick,
Perhaps a little more and another little lick.
I feel just like a child, so silly for being naughty,
So what if I'm fat - at least I'm not forty!

Sherrlee Blythin

MY KITCHEN

Sitting in my kitchen,
On my kitchen stools.
Playing silly beggars,
Acting stupid fools.
Sitting across the table,
Looking into your eyes,
My kitchen's full of capers,
Which is hardly a surprise,
Where's my coffee?

Susan Ann Thomas

PLAIN TALKING PLAIN EATING

I watch them making meals,
Everyday on our TV.
I carefully write the ingredients down,
And think to myself.
I'll make that for tea,
I dream about having a party.
With me as the perfect host,
Then I come back to earth with a bang,
I've burnt both the beans and the toast.
I'll try again tomorrow,
To make a dish that has class.
But when I tell my dear hubby,
He just looks up from his paper and snarls.
Don't go making ow't fancy,
I want a pan of thick tatti ash.
You can keep all them fancy meals,
With all them herb's, cream and wine.
Just give me a plate of plain grub,
And that lass will suit me fine.

Winifred Wardle

THE FEAST THAT CAUSED CHAOS

Sometimes I get it right
Other times I get it wrong
Armed with my apron on
I'll prepare a feast to give em all a treat
I'll mix the ingredients in a bowl
And beat, knead and stir as well
Soon it will all turn into superb
Cakes, biscuits and a casserole
And whilst making the chocolate cake
Who could resist a little taste
With doing this it looked like a ski slope
But it still tasted quite unique though

My wonderful creations are left
To cook, bake and rise while I clean up the bomb-site
And wipe the flour off my face
The table is set, I feel a little peckish
Some toast under the grill, have an omelette as well
The phone rings and it's a friend
I'm kept talking and disaster strikes!
The omelette sends the fire brigade out
The toast and biscuits are burnt to oblivion
Even the cake hasn't risen, the casserole wasn't cooked
'Cause I forgot to turn the oven on
Then another half-hour went by before I realised
It was still cold cause the oven had packed up!
Then to top it all off, my fella brings back,
A bottle of coke instead of a bottle of wine
So the cake was thrown and it landed
In a gooey mess on his face!

Vanessa Salt

COOK-ED HOUSE

My first attempt at cooking,
Was not a great success.
It ended up with leaving
My whole house in a mess.

For the bread I put in the toaster,
Burst into a big flame.
While my attention was elsewhere,
There was no one else to blame.

The smoke in that small kitchen,
Made it difficult to breathe.
So I opened up the outside door,
To give my breathing some relief.

But when I took this action,
The frying pan caught fire.
And the flames coming from the toaster,
They got even higher.

The Fire Brigade were quickly there,
Covering everything with foam.
But by the time they took this action,
I had nearly lost my home.

Danny Pyle

KITCHEN NIGHTMARE

Let's buy a new kitchen I brightly chirped,
It will make life easier and cut down on work.
With plenty of cupboards and a new worktop,
An insert sink and of course a new hob.

The kitchen's chosen and now we wait,
For the van to arrive on the delivery date.
Rooms piled high with bottles and tins,
Old bits of units, doors and hinge.

Follow instructions on how the units are built,
I think it would be easier to put on a kilt.
Just as you get the unit ready for assembly,
You look for the screws and find the box empty.

The plumber arrives to sort out the pipes,
Don't drain all the tank, was his advice.
He starts to arrange the pipes for connection,
He goes out to the van to bring a wrench in.

The water starts pouring out the loose pipe,
I walked in the room to find water at knee height.
I don't want a swimming pool, I cry in distress,
Turn off the water and let's clear up the mess.

Finally we put the last unit in place,
I am glad it's all over, couldn't keep up this pace.
A gleaming new kitchen, our pride and joy,
Couldn't go through this again whatever the ploy.

Fay Stanton

KITCHEN STAFF

People may not see our faces
But we must take many paces.
Up and down the stone floor kitchen,
Preparing all the cooking.
Bless our wonderful souls
We deserve so many goals.

The joy of all that jelly,
Rumbling in your bellies.
The enjoyable tea for Nelly,
While watching all that telly.

Throw some milk Cathy, dear
Oh, Moira you've slipped.
Up you get now, your wet on the rear
Quick old Martha is coming
Who spilt the milk.
I was told to just throw it,
So that's what I did.

Pass the spuds Ethel dear,
Oh, gosh all those eyes.
Berty boy, these are faggots,
Stuffing no, this is a haggis.

As you can see
We have some fun.
Training new ones
To feed your tums.
Hoping the rice doesn't stick to your gums,
For a refund you may have
Or join our happy gang.

Lena Hilton

THE KITCHEN FROM HELL

Beep, Beep, Beep,
The smoke alarm screams at me.
Flames emerging from the grill,
Help! I need another pill.
Have a look at the cookery book,
Oh, I wish that I could cook!
Children running round my feet,
Now I've gone and burnt the meat.
My pots and pans are boiling over,
Food stains cover my pullover.
To hungry mouths I serve it up,
Then I sit down with saucer and cup.
Why is there always a burning smell?
When I am in the kitchen from hell?

Dawn Kerr

HOW NOW BROWN COW

Never keep a budgerigar near a kitchen door,
You will regret it for evermore!
Quite clever, these little birds are,
Uttering words, even sentences, you
Would not dare to say.
To certain people coming your way!

I dropped my fresh pie in horror,
As my mother-in-law walked by, in rage!
Guess what the budgie said as she,
Cheerfully was passing his cage?
'How Now Brown Cow!'
I did not know whether to cry or laugh?

Then that was not enough,
The pie for tea on the floor.
Mother-in-law rather upset and sore!
As I apologised for the language,
Imagine then to my horror,
Cheerfully fluttering and chirping.
Loud and almost singing,
'You have done it now, done it now!'

This tiny bird's caper,
Raised more than steam and vapour!
Difficult to defuse, or even explain later.
I, have learned a lesson,
So take my advice.
Never teach a bird to sing or speak,
You never know, whom he'll meet and greet!

Anna Elliott

CAN COOK - WON'T COOK

This is dedicated to Marianne,
Who'll get out of cooking, if she can.
Help! Where is the spatterguard?
Frying things are really hard.
I've encouraged my darling daughter,
Who doesn't even burn the water.
When she tries, she's really good,
As next to the cooker, she is stood.
Getting down to making a cake,
The only thing she's happy to bake.
Cooking a joint or a chop,
Easy, as in the oven they'll pop.
To Jamie, a big 'well done,'
As Marianne, your heart has won.
You've really given us some cheer,
She'll never starve, as you are here.
Now we know that you can cook,
We won't have to buy her a book.

Josie Minton

DAY-DREAMING WITH KITCHEN AROMAS

In the kitchen you can find me many hours a day
But I am not a great cook I regret to have to say
I tend to be absent-minded so cooking can be a bind
And aromas in the kitchen really stir my mind
Aroma, aroma, a word not often heard
But it conjures up a picture finer than a word
Aroma of coffee beans or freshly baked bread
Aroma of lemon curd or vanilla spread
Aroma of peppermint, aniseed or ginger
Aroma of rum truffles or an almond finger
Aroma of brandy, kirsch or wine
Aroma of hops or whiskey fine
Aroma of onions frying in a pan
Aroma of bacon sizzling all it can
Aroma of beef roasting on a spit
Aroma of toast when it's burnt a bit

I'll make myself a coffee before I bake the bread
That will give me time for more thoughts in my head
Aroma, aroma, it's around us all the day
Do we take this sense for granted?
Perhaps many of us may

Maureen Stewart-Condron

VEGGIE FOR LIANE

So now you've hit the 'veggie' scene,
Pasta, cheese and dried mung beans.
A million tons of long grain rice,
Forty odd of Asian spice.
What's the food you like the most,
Brussell sprouts on buttered toast?
Or can you have for your tea,
A little fishy from the sea.
Perhaps grass 'sannies' they are good,
The best of all the 'veggie' food.
Carrots, spuds and cabbage all,
With celery, that's ten feet tall.
A mix and match of just a few,
Will give to you a 'veggie' stew.
While I still like to eat,
Piggies, sheep and fat cows' meat.
Maybe one day we'll be the same,
But I think 'veggies' feel the pain.
From the ground when they're pulled out,
And that's a lot to think about.

J S Liberkowski

THE TALE OF THE CREAMED FISH SOUP

I used to have a restaurant, I served 'European' type cuisine,
We had a German chef, an Italian waitress, the decor was a dream!
We prided perfect ion in all that we aspired, I couldn't wait to be 60,
Then I could be retired.
That and to make perfect puds was all that I desired,
Our hygiene was impeccable, our service? Nine out of ten, our wine list.
Small but discerning, well, it always pleased the men!
Our blackboard offered delectable delights to tempt most fickle appetites.
But the smoked mackerel hung about a bit so in the bin it was cast!
Our motto was 'If In Doubt . . . Chuck It Out' including some of our guests!
These were on our list as 'undesirable' along with mice and other pests!
Then came the night the undercover journalist dined! He gave us not a clue,
The fillet steak had also been 'chucked' as it was a little too blue!
As I only worked the lunch time shift I left old 'Klaus' in charge,
Little did I know how he despised my frugality.
For he'd secretly rescued both fish and steak! Tonight they were his 'special
Dishes of the day! Would my life ever achieve normality?
Our 'spy' ate with such gusto! The 'fillet Spitzen Singapore' he declared,
'Wunderbar!' The creamed fish soup?' Stupendous! I've never tasted anything
Quite like it before!'
We got five stars for food! 'Flavoursome and plenty.'
The rest was incidental, our conclusions elementary!
So the moral of this story is: When out to gourmet spies impress with
Succulent food ne'er seen,
Don't ask any questions of the fish or the steak . . .
You'll never know where they've been!

Joyce M Hefti-Whitney

IT'S A CHEF'S LIFE

What is this life if it is so fickle?
You have no time shallots to pickle.
And you spill the consommé from the ladle,
Before you get it to the table . . . from the cookpot.

You try to make a nice plum pie,
And build the centre very high.
Can't understand the criticism said,
Discover you used prunes instead . . . you're a crackpot.

And now, let's try to bake some bread,
You knead and knead till it's time for bed.
Forget the tins near the oven door,
It's risen all over the kitchen floor . . . use your loaf.

That streaky bacon's rather skinny,
Flat splashes all over your plastic pinny.
And don't expect to get a handshake,
For an omelette looking like a pancake . . . you're no egghead.

A simple dessert - a pink blancmange?
Resembles more of a bathroom sponge.
Your girlfriend made it - (cor! What a looker)
She let it boil all over the cooker . . . use Vim not vigour.

December's here - make a Christmas pud'n',
Mix it properly so it's no dud'n.
Take your time, take care, don't fiddle,
How could it collapse like that in the middle? . . . Give it to Santa.

As shown on telly, as a last resort,
At intervals, have a swig of port.
Something's making you feel quite dizzy,
And that spaghetti's looking fizzy! . . . Just forget it

Take that silly hat off and go back to being a motor mechanic . . .

Freda Baxter

TROUBLE ON THE STOVE

Delia said, 'Add salt, sugar, onion and rice,
And just before it comes to the boil add the allspice.
When finished it should be nice and fluffy.'
Standing over this stove is making me irritable and huffy.

This was meant to be fluffy white rice,
And I would not give the result to mice.
Let's find the page again in her cookbook,
Page ten, now let's take a deep breathe, be calm and have a closer look.

Delia said, 'Add flour, eggs, salt and make a well,'
Please, good heaven, in your kindness, cast a lucky spell.
It says, 'After thirty minutes it should be brown and tender.'
It's as hard as a rock, Oh hell, I've had it, I surrender!'

This was meant to be for my children's and visitor's tea,
It's almost four o'clock, oh miserable me!
Do I have time to dash out for more ingredients?
'Must tiptoe outside, I wouldn't like to shock and upset my visiting residents.

Delia said, 'If you fail, try a simpler approach,'
I can see Mrs Simms next door, not busy, but I'm afraid to encroach.
Take pot luck, I say and hope for the best,
The perfect cook, this is my humble quest.

Mrs Simms, as I was passing, gives me a knowing nod,
Has my cooking in the past always been so bad?
Clad in her frilly apron, humming and with intricate hands she achieves a perfect result,
For me to do this, I'd have to join an occult.

Delia said that we should all sit together and eat,
Fluffy rice, soft dumplings, lush greens and meat.
'Did you cook this delicious fare?' They in unison enquired,
'Forgive me, Miss Smith,' 'Of course, who else? I lied.

Margaret Andrews

AN APPLE TART TO MAKE

Kitchen sink clean and clear, work tops tidied up,
Preparation underway an apple tart to make.
Utensils selected carefully and cooker now switched on,
Abiding by the instructions from the cookery book by my side.

Ingredients chosen from the press in packets fresh and new,
Unopened presentation packs set upon the table top.
In wait of an incision with scissors to attack,
And pour into the bowl so large sitting there in wait.

Weighing scales! What are they? Oh yes, there in the press,
So brought then to the surface a function to perform.
And so pursue the required amounts of all that is in need,
To make an apple tart - at least that's what I thought.

So far so good, at least it seemed, the pastry now prepared,
Just to find the oven was not switched on at all.
But worse than that was to come - yes, I might add,
No apples in store, how could this be I couldn't understand.

An apple tart I think not, not this time for sure,
So from the press above my head mincemeat in a jar.
Now to capacity the pie was filled with the contents of the jar,
A surprise in store I thought with glee, nothing can go wrong.

For an hour or more the pie is sat within the oven there,
But nothing seemed to happen, no cooking seemed to be.
The oven, yes, it was switched on and heating, yes, it was,
But to my surprise the fan was gone so no tart of any kind.

Catherine O'Kane

FIT FOR A QUEEN

I opened the cupboard and looked for the book,
With glossy pictures that showed how to cook.
Apron donned I began to read,
About all the ingredients that I would need.
Four measures of this, a pinch of that,
A grease-proof tin, an ounce of fat.
I whisked the eggs, I weighed the flour,
I timed the oven to half an hour.
I creamed the mix in a plastic bowl,
Round and round then I made a hole.
To pour in the eggs and beat quickly,
To make a smooth consistency.
I sieved the flour and folded it in,
And dolloped it into the baking tin.
Then into the oven to slowly bake,
And transform into a beautiful cake.
But when the door was opened wide,
I stared in horror at what was inside.
No lovely sponge, no golden rise,
Instead a flat, nasty surprise.
The cake was crispy, black and thin,
And destined for the kitchen bin.
A smoking surface like the moon,
And as tempting as a stale prune
I cried aloud then began to laugh,
At the book's lovely photograph.
Then stared at the mess before my eyes,
And before the ruin I surmised,
That instructions in cook books must tell lies.

Katriona Hart

HAPPY KITCHEN HOURS

Although my kitchen is tiny,
I have lots of fun in there.
Making cakes and puddings for which I have a flair.
Sometimes I follow recipes from all my many books,
Other times I improvise like many other cooks.
It gives me lots of pleasure this cooking love of mine,
Hoping what I make will always turn out fine.
But sometimes things go wrong and very sad to say,
One year I made a Christmas cake and had to throw it all away.
The cake looked really lovely and was iced with loving care,
But when we came to cut it, it had gone so very hard.
It was impossible to eat.
So we had to say goodbye to our Xmas teatime treat,
Sometimes if a mishap should come your way
There is something you can do to save the day.
If a sponge cake for example sinks in the middle,
Just cut out that part and fill in with some fruit.
Decorate with cream and serve as a sweet,
The cake isn't wasted and you still have a treat.
Cakes and puddings are my favourites to bake,
But I do also cook other things as well.
As my neighbours who lunch with me can tell,
Sometimes it's casserole or maybe some fish.
Served with potatoes and vegetables to make a nice dish.
My kitchen ends up with pots and pans everywhere,
But I've really enjoyed all my time spent in there.

Shirley Talmadge

PANACEA

In the kitchen when doing the dishes,
We talk about Adler and Freud.
And the Libs and the Labs and the Tories,
And sometimes we get quite annoyed.

We talk about winning the Lottery,
And the fact that the rent's overdue.
And how we would spend all that money,
And the rota for cleaning the loo.

We talk of our friends and relations,
Of travel, the Royals and God.
Of surrogate mothers and condoms,
And virginity - though it seems odd!

We talk about Tracey's new lover,
And babies and nappies and prams.
We talk about getting employment,
And we *talk about* passing exams!

We talk of our needs and ambitions,
Our yearnings and innermost wishes.
And although you might think I am mad,
I look forward to doing the dishes!

Dave E Priest

CAN'T COOK . . . WILL COOK

Chilli con-coction, bolognause
Oh it's sticking to my jaws!
The wife's been on a cooking course . . .
There's no respite for me.
Swallow quickly you won't taste it,
But for goodness sake don't waste it.
Or she'll make it into sandwiches and serve it up for tea!

Now the gastric juices flow,
Just as well 'cause here we go.
With that jerry-built disaster
That is known as 'Cottage Pie'
You can't call it good nutrition.
Needs a writ for demolition,
And a stick of dynamite to blow the whole shebang sky-high!

Now it flapjack goodness gracious!
This takes guts, so be audacious.
As they're full of 'healthy goodness'
Such as wholemeal flour and bran,
She's left out the nuts and honey.
Make you fat and cost you money.
Brace yourself and grit your dentures: Face disaster like a man!

No more please . . . I just can't take it!
Though it took you hours to bake it.
Might I dare to recommend
That food taste better when it's canned.
Oh my chest! Has someone shot me?
Sure a bullets really got me!
Never criticise a woman with a rockbun in her hand!

Dorothy Kershaw

THE ABSENT-MINDED COOK

On Monday, I made apple pie,
To serve with home-made custard
Which looked alright, a yellow cream,
But tasted - yuk - of mustard!

On Tuesday night, our supper dish
Was bubbling (sweet) lasagne.
I'd shaken sugar in, not salt,
You just can't do that, can ya?

Wednesday's was a cheapo meal,
Just omelettes for our dinner.
But they were runny, pale, half raw.
That meal was not a winner.

When Thursday came around, we sat
Down to a feast of curry.
But I'd used too much vindaloo,
And they all left in a hurry.

On Friday I cooked fish and chips,
With home-made piccalilli.
A heavy hand with spice had made it
Fiery picca, silly!

Saturday breakfast, so we planned,
Was toast and Marmite spread.
Except I found the jar scraped clean,
Then went and burned the bread.

When Sunday came, I'd had enough
Of culinary disasters.
To crown it all, I cut my hand
And could I find the plasters?

Elizabeth Gwent

DISTRACTED

I've done the potatoes,
And cut them into chips.
Then the phone rings,
I chat until I hear the pips.

When I return,
The kitchen's full of smoke.
I forgot I'd put the chip pan on,
For incoming folk.

I open doors and windows,
To let out the smell.
Grab a damp cloth,
The fire to try and quell.

I manage to smother it,
But honestly to tell.
I'll never be distracted again,
I learnt my lesson well.

My poor little kitchen,
Did not look the best.
But when I've cleaned it up,
I can sit and rest.

Joyce Evans

KITCHEN CAPERS

One day I tried to be a cook,
My friends I tried to impress.
I went in the kitchen - had a look,
I couldn't believe the mess!

I phoned my mother to help me out,
She came round, like a shot.
She asked me: What's this all about?
I told her of my plot.

I thought that I would make a cake,
And ice it perfectly.
My friends didn't believe I could bake,
But in fact it wasn't me.

I had to admit to all of them,
It wasn't my creation.
Not only did I not bake the cake,
I didn't do the decoration!

Sue Butcher

MY NO JAM

The glass jars twinkled in the sun,
For hot, fruity jam they were waiting.
The fruit I had chosen was damson,
And my success I was highly rating.

I weighed and measured and stirred,
As the mixture boiled and bubbled.
Up on the wall the fan whirred,
By failure I was not troubled.

In a saucer the water was waiting,
To test the set of my jam.
The appetite it would be sating,
Of my brand-new husband Sam.

I proudly presented my prize,
Next day at the breakfast table.
I felt smug, efficient and wise,
Now jam to make I was able.

Sam unscrewed the lid and looked,
At the shiny, dark fresh preserve.
He loved everything I had cooked,
So more praise I did deserve.

He plunged in his knife to scoop,
Then looked at me in amazement.
I felt my smile start to droop,
As I stared at the blade, all bent.

There was no way to get the jam out,
Set like concrete it was.
Of one thing there was no doubt,
My jam was a solid, lost cause!

Laura Carlisle

MY CHOCOLATE CAKE

Today I am gong to attempt to bake,
And make myself a chocolate cake.
I've found a book with the recipe in,
So to bake my cake I shall begin.
I've weighed my flour, marg, cocoa and sugar,
And with the eggs I mix them together.
I pour out the mixture into a tin,
Then I open the oven and pop it in.
The cake to bake doesn't take long,
But when I go back it's all gone wrong.
My cake hasn't risen it's as hard as a rock,
It's that hard it could be a building block.
Instead of self-raising flour, I'd used plain,
And now I must start all over again.

Donna Dibb

SOMETHING COOKING

I wanted to do some baking,
Today I didn't have any flour.
I pop into my corner shop,
It must have took one hour.
When I got home and started to bake,
No margarine, no eggs, no meat,
No onions to put into my pie.
I think I'll do some chips have
Got plenty of potatoes in and as
For the home baked pie -
I'll get it from a tin!
It works out cheaper in the end,
Of that you can be sure.
It does not matter where it's from,
He always asks for more.

Julie Jones

KITCHEN FRIENDS

Our mum's got a freezer at home,
 - Yours too? - Well; so what?
Frozen chips, ice-lollies galore,
 - But, guess what else we've got?

A machine for making fizzy drinks!
 - not you too, you copy cat!
Something fishy here, me thinks!
No wonder us kids are fat!

Now, let me see, what else is there?
Oh yes; cod and chips in ten minutes flat.
Roast chicken 'flown' in by microwave . . .
Well - what do you think of that?

Tell me why then, my new friend,
Do I get a longing pang?
And all my pocket-money I'll spend,
 - on the 'chippie' and ice-cream vans!

Rosemary A V Sygrave

WHEN I GET HARASSED AT MEALTIME

My pie-crust is usually golden brown,
Acclaimed as being the best in town,
But it comes out crisp and black,
When I've got to have eyes in my back.
This type of cooking's not a bit like mine,
Except when I get harassed at mealtime.

Sausages making a sizzling sound,
The juiciest sausages for miles around,
But they split and they go bang,
And then they stick to the frying pan.
This type of cooking's not a bit like mine,
Except when I get harassed at mealtime.

Sugar in the salt cellar, gravy powder in the coffee,
I started making soufflé, but it turned out like toffee.
I peeled potatoes, put them on, I should have been in clover,
The kids are squabbling, the dog is barking and the spuds are boiling over,
This type of cooking's not a bit like mine,
Except when I get harassed at mealtime.

I am a good cook, I know I am,
I can make things like stew and jam.
Things turn out fine when I'm alone,
Just now and then my dumplings turn to stone.
This only happens when the kids come to dine,
I *love* to be harassed at mealtime.

Alan R Carson

KITCHEN CAPERS

I'm always in the kitchen, always doing chores,
Washing dishes, feeding fishes, polishing the floors.
My radio spits music, the kettle steams and splutters.
Pressure cooker hisses, my mouth is full of mutters.
An oven ready chicken defrosts inside a dish,
Poor fowl can't even scowl, but holds a bone to wish.
I mix the Yorkshire puddings, open up some peas,
Mash them into mushy ones, hope that no one sees.
The cooker's under pressure to cook dinner in a hurry,
If it burns I guess I'll learn to make a spicy curry.
I have a popping toaster, a microwave, a blender,
And once I've fed this family I'm going on a bender!
The dishes wait; anticipate. Will they be washed tonight?
Fairy liquid reads their minds, sympathising with their plight.
The yellow rubber gloves I have, protect my hands and fingers,
An extractor fan does all it can but cooking smells still linger,
The family have eaten now so it's time to stop my bitchin',
Switch off the light, say goodnight to you my loyal kitchen.

Margaret Scragg

BANGERS AND FLASH!

Everyone's favourite is Bangers and Mash,
An easy meal to make,
But there's never been one quite like it,
A dish to make you shake!

The evening was in November,
It was on Bonfire Night,
Dad was doing the cooking
And he gave us all a fright.

Fireworks were going off all around
The loudest bang came from down the hall,
The smell of smoke filled the air
Then hubby came in with a vacant stare.

'You should have seen the sausages
They flew right out of the pan,
The cooker ring exploded and caused a sudden flash,
But everything's ready as usual for,
teatime Bangers and Flash!'

Barbara Colman

PANCAKE ENCORE!

Shrove Tuesday I said I'd make pancakes
(like numerous years gone before)
it's becoming a family tradition,
'though I see it more as a chore.
The kitchen was cleared for my safety
(the sharp things were out of the way)
a recipe sat by the cooker,
in case I should somehow go astray.

I whisked up a mixture of promise,
then sieved out the lumps that I'd made
and heating the oil just a bit far,
thought of the Fire Brigade,
but holding my breath and the ladle,
I slowly allowed them to meet,
then gasped as I gulped in the black smoke
and wondered what else they could eat.

The pancakes with pancake aggression,
demanded to be overturned,
so I called in the family cheer team,
who'd been waiting with growing concern.
I took up the handle with courage,
counted slowly from one up to three,
then flicked up the dreadful concoction
and wondered where next it would be . . .

I promised to make them all pancakes
(like numerous years gone before)
and befitting the family tradition,
they landed in piles on the floor!

Angela Rogerson

AUNTY'S RECIPE FOR DISASTER

I went on a visit to aunty's, she lives out Cambridge way,
Very good with oil paints, and does a bit of cooking so they say,
A car was sent to collect me, I was going for lunch and tea,
What sort of day would I have, I supposed I must wait and see.

We arrived at aunty's just before noon, and she was really in a tizzy,
The mixture for the Yorkshire pud, had frothed up and gone fizzy,
She tipped it on the pastry board, then got the rolling pin,
I'd never seen batter rolled before, but then she'd been at the gin!

What a mess the kitchen was, there was batter splashed everywhere,
It had run down aunty's stockings, and she'd got plenty in her hair,
What was left she had to scrap, then set to and made another mixing,
This was of a different texture, looked ideal for wall tile fixing . . .

Aunty had earlier made a sponge, and asked me to put in the filling,
Well when one had been invited out, 'twas good manners to show willing,
Brandy flavoured butter icing; to give it body I thought I'd whisk it,
What a shock when I saw the sponge, it was no thicker than a biscuit

I had to ask my dear old aunt, what had gone wrong with her sponge,
She said it must have been the eggs, that had turned the mixture into gunge.
I never said another word, as we stood there on the river bank,
Feeding aunty's sponge to the ducks, who as they ate it slowly sank.

Wenn The Pen

MICROPHOBIA

My mother bought a microwave,
She saw it as a must.
It sits upon the worktop,
Gathering the dust.

It's only got two dials to turn,
Not difficult to use.
So why is it still gleaming white?
It hasn't blown a fuse.

They're scared of it, my mum and dad,
'It's too high-tech' for oldies'.
I've tried to help them understand,
The 'waves' heat up the coldies.

My dad, he put some gravy in,
Just the other week.
He gave it three whole minutes
Then he went to have a peek.

It wasn't hot enough for him,
And he became quite troubled.
So he put it in a saucepan
And cooked it 'til it bubbled.

I showed him how to heat baked beans,
He looked on, clearly pleased.
I phoned him up the other day,
'How is *it* now?' I teased.

'We'd like you to have it, Helen dear,
It was an impulse buy.
We don't like these new fangled things,
Still, you don't know unless you try.'

Now I've got their new microwave
And I've become much posher,
So I'm trying to persuade them next
To purchase a dishwasher!

Helen M Lambourne

THE KITCHEN
(where angels fear to tread)

A haven of peace where the family ne'er tread
But for moments of weakness to look for the bread.
I'm sure they can't see me, it's like camouflage
A solitary figure midst packets and jars.
They call from their vantage points all round the house
But if I stay quiet they pester my spouse.
I'm safe in the knowledge, if I close the doors,
They won't cross the threshold for fear of the chores.
In here I hold court, queen of all I survey
But lest I forget, it's a job with no pay.
Sometimes when I'm lonely and yearn for my brood
If they keep their distance, I bribe them with food.
But when they're in trouble and one of them's hurt
Or with some trepidation they ask 'Where's my shirt?'
I make them so welcome and offer them tea
Then gently remind them, *admission is free . . .*

Lynda M Bourne

LEARNING TO COOK

In the kitchen I have no fun
except for making cakes an' the odd cherry bun

When we talk about cooking, it is meant to be
a thing which to me should come naturally

Yet how come everything I touch, should burn or disintegrate in its
container

I have had many a teacher, and I have tried to learn
Yet only the other day I opened a can of beans and just my luck they
ran away

As through the door they passed I heard them say
'we're sorry wee lass'

So even if I did learn to cook and not to burn,
who's to say that the ingredients I'm using will not run away.
I suppose it is just down to me at the end of the day.

Nadia Darwish

YOUR COOKER

I am your cooker
So keep me clean
When you have finished
Give me 'Mr Sheen'
Clean me up as good as gold
For I don't want to grow old
I am here to give you joy
I am here to give you treats
So when you've made yourself a treat
Don't forget I need a sweep.

Hyacinth M Sweeney

THE NON-STICK PAN

Yesterday, I bought a frying pan, 'non-stick' the label said,
I brought it home, all full of go, and put it on the hob,
I cracked two eggs into a bowl, and tossed them in the pan
Well aware that in the shop, 'non-stick' the logo ran.

Well, the eggs they burned and fried and stuck,
I got in a terrible mess.
I threw the pan out of the door, and the dogs they ate the rest.
I took it back up to the store, a refund for to get,
The lady on the till, she said, 'We've not had one brought back yet'.

I got my money back quite quick, and now what shall I do
Dispense with omlettes, and fried eggs, I think I'll do a stew!

Patricia Fryer

UNTITLED

This time, you are stuck with a single sweet dish.
Eat with cream or custard, whichever you wish.
It is not high in calories, and is simple to make.
And will do you more good than that gooey cream cake.

I hope that you are eating the things that are nice.
And sticking to my recipes, which give good advice.
Healthy eating does not mean you have to break the bank.
You can eat well, and stay slim, without becoming a crank.

When tying your laces, can you see your shoes?
If you can't, then I think, some weight you should lose.
Follow my recipes, and get your weight down.
And instead of the bus, you will feel like walking into town.

W Winton

CINDY'S SNACK

A few years ago on our
washing day, Cindy our
puppy was not in my way.

It was one Friday afternoon
my husband was out and would
be home soon.

When he got home and put the
bag on the floor we went to
put things away this is what I am
about to say.

Cindy went into the bag where
two meat and potato pies and
vanilla slices were and thought
to herself 'hm, I'll have these for
supper'. Whilst our backs were
turned she scoffed the lot.
Has she done it again?
I think not.

Nicola Regan

GOURMET SPLASH

Our kitchen is a battlefield. All trespassers beware!
The war-torn zone will detonate, so handle with good care.
It started with a pancake that surpassed all other heights
And left a lasting hallmark of its tossing on the lights.
Don't ask me why our soufflés fade away and always flop -
How champagne corks make Morse code ceiling signals when they pop -
I'm still in pain negotiating salmon cooked in plaster
And grudgingly admit that too much salt leads to disaster.

Thrice charred, we turn our backs on tempting morsels for the grill
And veto awkward cartons that erupt and tend to spill
For 'Mr X Disgusted' - and defeated by a spout -
Propelled one through the window and the milk came gushing out
My leaded lights in smithereens, but, gratified, the cat
Still licks his lips expecting flying saucers on his mat.

Our Waterloo could well have been a gastronomic fling
It's-easy-once-you-know-how ('til you go and burn the thing)
The taste buds sizzled. 'Omelette flambé' Um! Of that I'm certain
Until it set alight and made a beeline for the curtain.

The firemen arrived in time and siphoned my new dress
I glimpsed at the burnt offering and fainted under stress.
By then we were a laughing stock. News of our kitchen capers
Had made the headline 'Gourmet Splash' in all the local papers.

So now we dream of luxuries like finger-lickin' chips
And live a flameless life avoiding culinary blips
We've ripped up all the cook books making showers of confetti
And plan a new best seller 'How to thrive on tinned spaghetti'.

Sylvia Howell Williams

TUESDAY MORNINGS

Every week I would look forward to Tuesday morning
Around nine thirty I listened for the bell to ring.
An exuberant two year old was ready to cook
Her recipes didn't need to come from a book.

Apron on, then into the bowl went flour and salt
Did some go on the floor, well that was the spoon's fault!
Slowly it was mixed with water almost drop by drop
Meant the pleasure lasted longer - so why stop.

The china rolling pin was out I knew in a flash
Years ago my son had let one roll to the floor - smash.
So I thought a piece of very thick doweling stick
Well sandpapered each end for Christine would do the trick.

Using a wide bladed knife the bowl had a good scrape
Now came the best part, choosing and pressing out each shape
Soon the cooked dough was left to cool on a wire tray
Then it was ready to paint and continue our play.

Mary E Beale

CLANGERS IN THE KITCHEN

This poem is about my kitchen,
That is the theme of this song,
It has got to be the most interesting room,
Especially when things go wrong.

Like mum's attempt at making bread,
The loaf was harder than a brick wall.
So we took it out the garden
And used it as a football.

Dad's home-made strawberry wine
Which almost blew the kitchen apart
It came out of the bottle just like a fountain
Or as if the bottle had a heart.

Aunty Rose's strawberry blancmange,
So hot it melted the mould
It gracefully sank until it was flat
And into the sink it rolled.

The toaster with the wonky spring
Which fired toast into the air
One piece landed in the bin
The other landed on my hair.

Every kitchen has stories to tell
And every one is unique
Some are so hilarious
You laugh until you are weak.

Eifion Thomas

THE PROOF IS IN THE EATING

One day I made an apple pie.
I put it in to cook.
The minutes passed, I waited.
At last I took a look.
It had risen to perfection,
A golden, crispy, brown.
I removed it from the oven,
And turned to set it down.
Just then my little dog appeared,
Barked, and made me jump.
The pie fell to the kitchen floor,
A mangled, sticky, lump.
I threw my hands up in dismay,
I shouted out '*Oh, no!*'
At which point all the family,
Arrived to watch the show.
Then, deftly, wielding knives and spoons,
They scraped up every bit,
And dumping it into a bowl,
Picked out the hair and grit.
They all said it would be a shame,
To see it go to waste.
So as I sat there open mouthed,
They dived in for a taste.
And very soon we all agreed,
That pastry would take some beating.
The proof of any apple pie,
Is always in the eating.

B J Ashenden

FOOD STUFFS

My cooking skills are doubtful this cry is from the heart
A full-size pudding starts off fine but finishes just part.
My cakes just sink, the meat goes dry, the gravy looks so sad
I wonder why I even try when everything seems bad.

The book says this, the book says that, the photo looks divine,
I follow everything I read and hope success is mine
But no, this time I've burnt it all, this gourmet meal for two
So once again, it's beans on toast - or anything will do.

With heavy heart one day I try to make just one more meal
I'll try a casserole, I think, it's easy, no big deal.
But, dear oh dear, the meat is tough the gravy one big lump.
The cat runs off, the fam'ly too - to take it to the dump.

So now we feast our eyes upon the television fayres,
They're perfect, and let's face it are worth watching from our chairs.
One day I'll have another try to make a perfect meal.
But not just yet, I can't explain, it's just the way I feel.

Zena A Horton

GRANDMA'S KITCHEN

Grandma's kitchen was her pride and joy,
Yorkshire range a-gleaming,
Granddad came in from his gardens one night,
With a sack, his face was beaming.

Now we were used to his offerings, fresh dug up,
A nice turnip perhaps for tea,
But that night as he tipped out his precious prize,
Fresh veggies were not to be.

A dozen chicks spilled out that bag,
A veritable swarm,
'We'll sit them by the fire dear,
Keep them nice and warm'.

The chickens, mind, had other ideas,
They soon were everywhere,
In cupboards, food and coal scuttle,
Some making for the stairs.

My grandma's face turned a shade of puce,
'Get them chickens out of here',
'I will when they've grown up a bit',
'In about three weeks my dear'.

By now she's getting mighty cross,
Her ample bosoms heaving,
Her pinny seeming to inflate,
Eruptive rages seething.

Thus ensued a mighty row,
The chickens joining in,
Shouting, squawking, feathers flying,
What an awful din.

'Enough', said grandma, calming down,
'Here is what we'll do',
It's them or me, you'll have to choose'.
'All right my dear, I'll think it through'.

Gail Guest

KITCHEN CAPERS

Please don't ask me to cook,
I will get on my knees and beg,
The chef of the house is you
Why, I can't even boil an egg.

Remember the last dinner party
I felt so sad and distraught,
I went by the book like it said
That proves it wasn't my fault.

Smoke poured out of the oven
The air was thick like fog,
The cat got splashed with gravy
And I twice fell over the dog.

I greeted the guests with drinks
Champagne on a crystal tray,
It wobbled and smashed to the ground
Your slippers were in the way.

I shuffled in with the dinner
It should have been ready at eight.
Everyone stared in silence
At the food squashed on their plate.

The oyster soup was frothy
We chewed our steak like gum,
The peas were really salty
And the pasta underdone.

I smiled through the icy gateaux
It was left for hours to thaw,
I offered them mints and coffee
But they scarpered out the door.

So please don't ask me to cook, 'cause that'll be the day
I'm happy to collect and pay for your choice of take-away.

Julie Botley

THE LOSING BATTLE

Everyone comes into the kitchen,
When I am trying to get a meal,
And if I should object, they say,
'Get with it, Mum, you're so unreal!'

Before I can begin to cook,
I have to find a working space,
Removing all the odds and ends
That have littered up the place.

There are letters, bills and abundant junk mail,
And seedlings on the window sill,
Together with the home-made wine
Fermenting, which I dare not spill!

Eventually, I start to make
The family's favourite fudge dessert,
But then one wants to use the sink,
And another wants to iron a skirt.

So bit by bit, the family drift
Into my kitchen once again,
They claim, 'togetherness means home'.
How can I really want to complain?

B Gordon

A DISASTER IN THE KITCHEN

Cooking wasn't a strong point of mine,
I never really had the time.
So one day I decided to learn,
but everything just seemed to burn.

Rock cakes hard enough to chip a tooth,
washing-up piled to the roof.
Bread as hard as a wooden log,
I couldn't even tempt our dog.

'Simple' was what I really needed,
but 'no more' the family had pleaded.
Yet after a week and some help from Kelly,
I succeeded in making some jelly.

I'm still no gourmet chef or cook,
but armed with my recipe book
with practice, patience and some time,
my cooking now turns out quite fine.

Susannah Bennett

HOW D'YA LIKE YOUR TORTOISE, BOILED OR FRIED?

A tortoise died - someone cried, they wanted to keep the shell.
They approached my mum for ideas, they wanted it shiny - no smell.
It was buried in the garden and left there to decay,
to assist the result mum tried another way.

This deceased tortoise was slowly simmered in a cooking pot
Shrinking the body, poking it out the holes was faster than leaving it to rot.
Our kitchen smelt disgusting - just as my boyfriend decided to call
when invited to stay for dinner suddenly was not hungry at all!
Intrigued by the stench he lifted the lid and looked inside -
when he saw the body 'cooking' there, his mouth fell open wide.

This way of 'doing tortoise' did not work at all well
- it ruined a good saucepan and buggered up the shell.
I won't go into details but it did look somewhat odd,
so poor old tortoise was laid to rest again underneath the sod.

It all sounds rather gruesome, but there is a positive side -
it didn't frighten my boyfriend off, in fact he took me for his bride.
We've never owned a tortoise, for a pet we'll never look -
but stenches often fill our kitchen,
'cause I'm such a rotten cook!

Nickie Manolescue

THE WRONG JOB

I hate to start out by bitchin'
But I loathe my work in the kitchen.
No matter how hard I try,
To boil, bake or fry,
I just can't produce meals with no hitch in!

I've practised again and again,
From exotic to simple and plain;
But I'm no good with a hob,
So I've got the wrong job,
I must change soon or end up insane.

P Sharratt

YOGHURT AND COFFEE

Hello yoghurt sitting there,
Shall I taste you, should I dare,
I think I will, as hunger strikes,
Wow! Weren't you nice, yoghurt there.

Hello coffee sitting there,
Wow! I'm thirsty, should I dare,
Yes I will, but will you mix,
Oh! I don't care, coffee there.

Now my tongue in my mouth,
Is dry again, as you do mix,
But time I give as you digest,
That silly yoghurt coffee mix.

Mary Jo West

KITCHEN CAPERS

The oven shelf was bowed and bent
and our dinner was not to be heaven sent.
For a steak and kidney pie I had slid
into the oven complete with the lid.
Potatoes and veg were ready in a pan
when all of a sudden there was an almighty bang.
At once my heart to the floor had sank
as the tin gave out its final clank.
Shakily I opened the oven door
to find dinner spread from top to floor.
This highlighted my fears and all that I dread
The dinner was replaced by egg instead.

Beatrice Jackson

FUDGE TOFFEE

We made fudge toffee, my brother and I,
Aunty had made some and it was swell,
If she could do it, so could we
With a lasting supply of sweets as well.

When mum was out we raided the larder -
2 oz of butter, 2 tablespoons of syrup,
2 oz of sugar, a tin of condensed milk,
And boil together until 5 mins is up.

The aroma was strong and finger-licking sweet,
Then we found mum's baking tray to grease,
We poured in the bubbling stickiness
And couldn't wait to try a piece.

We left it under the bed to cool,
But when we came to break it away,
The toffee had set just like concrete
And we couldn't get it out of the tray.

So we borrowed dad's chisel and hammer
But the toffee was as hard as sin,
We managed to break it in pieces,
But we made awful holes in the tin.

The time that we made fudge toffee -
It took hours to suck and chew,
And mum went spare when she saw the tray
And the spoon and pan stuck like glue.

Esme Francis

MRS FEATHER

Now, what was it I thought about
And said 'I shan't forget'?
The fact is I'm in awful doubt,
But I'll remember yet.

Ah yes! I left the gas on,
Just a while, to cut a rose,
But soon the smell of drifting smoke
Came by and hit my nose!

There are two things one can't ignore,
The milk-pan and the toast,
Or there'll be endless cleaning,
And chores I hate the most.

He's coming down for breakfast -
A voice rings out in pain -
'What are you doing, woman?
Burnt offerings again!'

Flora A Byford

INFORMATION

We hope you have enjoyed reading this book - and that you will continue to enjoy it in the coming years.

If you like reading and writing poetry drop us a line, or give us a call, and we'll send you a free information pack.

Write to

Arrival Press Information
1-2 Wainman Road
Woodston
Peterborough
PE2 7BU